Cho
Cherished

BECOMING *the* BRIDE *of* CHRIST

CHOSEN AND CHERISHED

BECOMING *the* BRIDE *of* CHRIST

EDNA ELLISON

JOY BROWN

KIMBERLY SOWELL

NEW HOPE
PUBLISHERS
Birmingham, Alabama

New Hope® Publishers
P. O. Box 12065
Birmingham, AL 35202-2065
www.newhopepublishers.com

New Hope Publishers is a division of WMU®.

Library of Congress Cataloging-in-Publication Data

Ellison, Edna.
  Chosen and cherished : becoming the bride of Christ / Edna Ellison, Joy Brown, and Kimberly Sowell.
     p. cm.
  ISBN 978-1-59669-271-8 (sc)
  1. Marriage--Religious aspects--Christianity. 2. Spirituality. I. Brown, Joy, 1946- II. Sowell, Kimberly. III. Title.
  BT706.E45 2009
  248.4--dc22
                            2009003260

ISBN-10: 1-59669-271-5
ISBN-13: 978-1-59669-271-8

N094152 • 0609 • 4M1

Dedication

To our heavenly Bridegroom who blessed us
with our earthly bridegrooms:
Snow Ellison (Edna's late husband),
Wayne Brown,
and Kevin Sowell.

TABLE OF CONTENTS

ACKNOWLEDGMENTS

uthors do not write books as islands standing alone. They owe many people thanks for their help in a labor of love such as this Bible study. Especially when three authors are coordinating their work, there is a sense of community as all the pieces come together under God's direction.

We—Joy Brown, Edna Ellison, and Kimberly Sowell—owe a debt of gratitude to the following competent staff at New Hope Publishers: Dr. Andrea Mullins, publisher, who believed in us as we received a contract and began our work; Joyce Dinkins, managing editor, who was an inspiration and guide for the project; and Randy Bishop, our hard-working editor, who supervised the details and helped design this Bible study in many ways with wise advice.

We also wish to thank the graphic designer, Sherry Hunt, who provided creative ideas for every page of this lovely book. Also we owe many thanks to copy editor Carolyn Goss, for catching our mistakes and making us look good. Jonathan Howe, marketing and sales manager, and Ashley Stephens, publicity and advertising specialist, have given many hours of service in the promotion and publicity for this book.

We are also compelled by love to thank original members of Women by Design—Marie Alston, Cherie Nettles, and Tricia Scribner, who inspired an earlier version of this study, *Here Comes the Bride of Christ*, from which this book was birthed.

Most of all, we thank God for being our Savior, Creator, and Friend. As part of the church, the bride of Christ, we proclaim our love for the heavenly Bridegroom and acknowledge Him as Lord of our lives.

CHAPTER ONE

FOUNDATIONS OF LOVE

By Joy Brown

ood news! As a believer, you are chosen by God the Father to be wed to His Son Jesus Christ. You're loved so deeply that on the Cross of Calvary He accomplished everything necessary to make you His bride. You're chosen and cherished!

The Bible is God's love letter to His bride, we who form the church. Using Paul's language, we are *"promised...to one husband, to Christ"* (2 Corinthians 11:2). As you go through this study, we hope you'll be amazed to see how many of Jesus's teachings, and many other passages of the Bible, are "wedding talk." Using

the marriage of a man and a woman as a symbol, God beautifully illustrates what it means for us to be in an intimate relationship with Christ.

The significance of what *chosen and cherished* means will be revealed throughout this book. In chapters 2–10, I encourage you to take time to do the Bible study activities, **"Love-Letter Bouquets,"** scattered throughout each chapter as they will reinforce and enhance the beautiful truths waiting to unfold. You will also find **"Reflections"** questions that are designed to stimulate further thinking on the chapter's topics. A special prayer ends each chapter accompanied by a highlighted **"Insights"** element that provides a story, poem, or interesting facts to spur further thought.

This first chapter is foundational to an understanding of what it means to be the bride of Christ and the key to the rest of this study. While you may find later chapters more meaningful than others — depending on your life experiences — we believe studying them in succession (unless led by the Holy Spirit to do otherwise) will build a beneficial bridge of understanding. Also, bear in mind that the customs we refer to in the study span the entire Bible.

It is possible that at different times and places throughout biblical history they differed. However, we are confident that most biblical scholars would concur with the general premises upon which we have based this book.

As these words are being written—and as you will later read them—the authors are continuing to lift prayers to God for you. We pray that before this study is complete, you'll recognize how much and how intimately you're loved by Jesus Christ—the blessed Bridegroom. May God bless you as you begin to make your wedding plans for eternity!

Before we study specific aspects of the wedding customs of biblical times in depth, it is important to have a general overview and definition of the several elements involved in the marriage process. What follows in this chapter is such an overview and will serve as the foundation for the remaining chapters in the book. (Here I would like to acknowledge Zola Levitt, a Jewish believer and teacher, whose little book, *A Christian Love Story*, provided an introduction and valuable insights into this chapter.)

The Betrothal

The betrothal, somewhat similar to our period of engagement, involved a serious commitment. In fact, a betrothed couple was legally married, accepting the liabilities and the assets of the other person. However, they could not consummate the marriage or be in each other's presence until after the wedding.

The betrothed bride was expected to remain faithful to her bridegroom. If she did not, the bridegroom had three choices. He could marry her anyway, have her stoned to death, or break the betrothal through a documentation of divorce.

When Joseph found out that Mary was expecting, he assumed she'd been unfaithful. He loved her too much to have her killed, yet being a man of integrity, he could not proceed with the marriage. He decided to break the betrothal privately. Then, an angel appeared to him, assuring him that the child within her was conceived of the Holy Spirit. (See Matthew 1:18–20).

Several steps were involved in betrothal. The next few chapters of this book examine these steps and how they relate to our lives today. Each one has a beautiful spiritual counterpart that will bless and inspire us.

CHOOSING THE BRIDE

The father of the bridegroom usually had responsibility for the first step in the betrothal process, which was initiating the selection of a suitable bride. (He may have listened to his son's preferences, but he was not obligated to follow them). The father would accompany his son to the home of the prospective bride and meet with her family.

God the Father has chosen you to be spiritually wed to His Son, Jesus: *"One of the seven angels...said to me, 'Come, I will show you the bride, the wife of the Lamb'"* (Revelation 21:9).

Before we get into the other aspects of the biblical marriage, let it be noted that when we refer to the *"bride of Christ," "our Bridegroom,"* and similar terms, we apply them to those who have in faith come into relationship with Him. As with any proposal, for a couple to become engaged the proposal has to be accepted. Our sincere prayer is that if you have never done so, this study will be the catalyst that brings you into relationship with Him. (See chapter 4, "Accepting God's Proposal," on page 53. Also see the conclusion, "A Wedding Invitation," starting on page 127.)

Marriage Contract

The bridegroom and his father went to the potential bride's home and presented a marriage contract to her and her father, to be read before at least two witnesses. The contract, or covenant, contained the promises and provisions concerning what the groom would do for his bride as her husband: *"For no matter how many promises God has made, they are 'Yes' in Christ"* (2 Corinthians 1:20).

Bride-price

The bridegroom paid the bride's father to marry his daughter. If the bridegroom was poor and couldn't pay with money, he could pay through acts of service (as when Jacob worked for Laban to marry Rachel — see Genesis 29:14–30).

Christ purchased His bride with His own sacrificial blood. *"Be shepherds of the church of God, which he bought with his own blood"* (Acts 20:28).

The Cup of Acceptance

The bridegroom poured a cup of wine and drank half of it. If the bride accepted his proposal, she drank the rest of the cup. From that time on, whenever the bride was out in public, she wore a veil to show that she was "set apart" for her bridegroom.

Each time we partake of communion, we are confirming that we have drunk Jesus's cup of acceptance: *"Then he took the cup, gave thanks and offered it to them, saying, 'Drink from it, all of you. This is my blood of the covenant, which is poured out for many for the forgiveness of sins'"* (Matthew 26:27–28).

Bridal Gifts

Once both sides had accepted the provisions of the covenant, the bridegroom gave special gifts, such as jewelry, spices, oils, or even money to his bride. These gifts were to help her prepare for the wedding.

Chosen and Cherished

Jesus has given His bride the gifts of the Spirit to help us prepare for our wedding: *"But each man has his own gift from God; one has this gift, another has that"* (1 Corinthians 7:7).

PREPARING THE BRIDAL CHAMBER

Once the proposal had been accepted, the bridegroom returned to his father's house, allowing time for him and his bride-to-be to prepare separately for their future life together. Essentially, he left his bride-to-be with a promise (whether spoken or not) that echoes Jesus's words, *"I am going to prepare a place for you. And . . . I will come back and take you to be with me"* (John 14:2–3).

Jesus gave His bride this beautiful promise in John 14:1–4. Please read and reread those words with great expectation.

The Wedding

THE DAY AND HOUR

The father of the groom supervised the progress of the bridal chamber, and he was the sole judge of when the project was finished. And, remember, this was no simple task for the groom. As Levitt writes, "The bridal chamber had to be beautiful — one doesn't honeymoon just anywhere; and it had to be stocked with provisions since the bride and groom were going to remain inside for seven days." Once the preparations were finished (usually around a year after the betrothal), the groom's father would give the OK for his son to go and get his bride for the wedding ceremony.

Likewise, only God knows when Jesus will come for His bride: *"No one knows about that day or hour, not even the angels in heaven, nor the Son, but only the Father"* (Matthew 24:36).

THE WATCHFUL BRIDE

Although the bride didn't know when her bridegroom would come, she watched for signs to see how the work on the bridal chamber was progressing. She remained in a constant state of readiness.

In the same way, the bride of Christ must live expectantly for the day when our Bridegroom will come to take us home with Him: *"Therefore keep watch, because you do not know on what day your Lord will come"* (Matthew 24:42).

THE WEDDING GARMENTS

As the bride discerned the time of her groom's return was near, she prepared her garments, making certain they were fresh and clean. Then she either laid them beside her or hung them in such a way that they would not get wrinkled. She made sure they were ready for the surprise wedding.

We too are to keep ourselves pure for that day. *"His bride has made herself ready. Fine linen, bright and clean, was given her to wear.' (Fine linen stands for the righteous acts of the saints)"* (Revelation 19:7–8). Further, the apostle John sees the wedding of the Lamb at the end of time as *"the Holy City, the new Jerusalem, coming down out of heaven from God, prepared as a bride beautifully dressed for her husband"* (21:2).

THE PROCESSIONAL

When the bridegroom's father gave the command (usually around midnight), the bridegroom gathered his friends. They marched through the streets carrying oil lamps, blowing the *shofar*, a ram's horn trumpet, and shouting, "The bridegroom comes!" When they arrived at the bride's home, the bridegroom waited eagerly in the street for her to come out to meet him. Accompanied by her family and friends, they proceeded to the place of the wedding.

One day we, too, will hear a shout, the sound of a trumpet, and our Bridegroom will come for us. We must remain ready to meet Him: *"At midnight the cry rang out: 'Here's the bridegroom! Come out to meet him!'"* (Matthew 25:6).

THE CEREMONY

At the conclusion of the ceremony, the couple once again shared a cup of wine from a common cup. We can prepare here on earth for the day we will share the experience of the common cup in His presence. The night before His death, Jesus gave us words to help us prepare for that day: *"I will not drink of this fruit of the vine from now on until that day when I drink it anew with you in my Father's kingdom"* (Matthew 26:29).

The Celebration

THE CONSUMMATION

After the ceremony, the couple entered the bridal chamber, usually for seven days. The purpose of this time was to get to know each other intimately and grow in understanding of each other.

The best man waited outside the door of the chamber. The groom informed him when the marriage had been consummated, and the waiting guests rejoiced for the couple had now entered into blood covenant with each other: *"The bride belongs to the bridegroom. The friend who attends the bridegroom waits and listens for him, and is full of joy when he hears the bridegroom's voice"* (John 3:29).

This physical custom points to a spiritual truth. One day we will come to know our Bridegroom intimately and only then will we be able to fathom His wondrous love for us.

THE MARRIAGE SUPPER

At the end of the seven days, the couple emerged from the bridal chamber. A great feast was given to celebrate the marriage of the bridegroom to his bride.

All that happens in our lives on earth is preparing us for the day we see our Bridegroom face-to- face, go to live in the home He has prepared for us, and experience the depths of His love:

> *"Let us rejoice and be glad and give him glory! For the wedding of the Lamb has come, and his bride has made herself ready. Fine linen, bright and clean, was given her to wear.... Then the angel said to me, 'Write, "Blessed are they who are invited to the wedding supper of the Lamb!"' And he added, 'These are the true words of God.'"*
> —Revelation 19:7–9

I AM MY BELOVED'S

As you can see, the wedding customs of biblical times are filled with beautiful imagery correlating to our lives as the bride of Christ. The imagery may seem unusual or unfamiliar at times, but don't be thrown off by it. As you study each chapter, the corresponding truths for today's living will become clear.

"And they lived happily ever after" is more than the closing line of a fairy tale. It is a reality for those who enter into covenant relationship with the Bridegroom, Jesus Christ. *"My beloved is mine and I am his"* (Song of Songs 2:16 NKJV).

PRAYER & PRAISE
JOURNAL

CHAPTER TWO

CHOSEN AND CHERISHED
By Edna Ellison

My then 11-year-old daughter Patsy and her friend Allison spent one afternoon planning their weddings. Each would be a bridesmaid in the other's wedding. One would ride in a limousine; the other in a carriage drawn by a white horse. They chose  décor, music, and food for their future nuptials. Each of the girls was missing only one ingredient: a future bridegroom who would choose her, ask her to marry him, and promise to cherish her forever.

Like Patsy and Allison, did you plan wedding details years ahead? Did you rehearse in dress-up lace and tulle, pretending you were solemnly promenading down the aisle? Did you, like most little girls, envision your future groom to be a perfect Prince Charming, an image no man could ever fulfill? Behind the make-believe lies this truth: every woman yearns to be chosen and cherished.

More important than our relationship with our earthly husband is our lasting relationship with Jesus Christ, the Bridegroom who loves His bride, the church. If you're a Christian, that's you! You're a part of the body of Christ, His church, whom Jesus, the Bridegroom, has chosen and cherished.

SIX PRINCIPLES OF BEING CHOSEN AND CHERISHED

The Bible is full of wedding imagery. Old and New Testaments refer to God as the strong bridegroom who loves unconditionally, rescues His bride (His people, the church), and takes her to a home in heaven. (See, for instance, Isaiah 54:5; Jeremiah 3:14 and 31:32; Ephesians 5:32; Revelation 19:7–9 and 21:2). From the Bible we have at least six reasons to assure us as Christ followers we've been chosen and cherished as the bride of Christ.

1. *God gives His promises in writing (John 20:31).*

When I met my future husband Snow, a handsome young man whose family had moved into our neighborhood, our relationship clicked right away. Then he went to a neighboring state for a two-week National Guard training assignment. I missed him more than anyone else I'd ever cared about. He wrote beautiful love letters every day. Saving the letters in a box under my bed, I often reread every precious word, especially his promise that he'd never leave me, regardless of anyone who tried to separate us.... I wondered if he meant those serious words.

Even the best men (and women) sometimes write words they don't mean. Often their promises fade, but God's promises never fail (Isaiah 40:8).

In Bible times the father of the groom chose a suitable wife for his son. He made all the arrangements and drew up a marriage contract, called *ketubah.* After he made sure the ketubah was agreeable to both families, it was offered to the bride. If she accepted it, she and the groom had to sign it before at least two witnesses. Following the reading of the ketubah before witnesses, it became a legal, binding contract.

Like the ancient bridegroom's father, God establishes a contract, a covenant, with us, the bride of Christ. He gives—*in writing*—His wonderful promises guaranteeing His truth. The Bible is a collection of love letters from the Lord. *"But these* [words recorded in the Bible] *are written that you may believe that Jesus is the Christ, the Son of God, and that by believing you may have life in his name"* (John 20:31, author's words in brackets). God tells us in writing that Jesus is His Son, the Messiah, our Bridegroom, who, incredibly, loved us enough to die for us. Yes, Snow wrote me love letters to tell me who he was and to assure me that his love was sincere, but God had set a precedent years before, providing His written promises of eternal love.

Chosen and Cherished

Love-Letter Bouquet

Pause to cherish God's promises for your life. As a groom gives his bride flowers, Christ gives you His holy words to savor. Think of each verse as a flower to add to your spiritual bouquet. As you answer questions about the verses, allow the Holy Spirit's aroma to sweeten your heart and touch your inner spirit.

Compare John 20:31 to 1 John 5:13–15. How do you *know* that you have eternal life?

Read Isaiah 40:8. Has anyone given you flowers that faded fast? How do flowers symbolize earthly love? What is the nature of God's love?

Reflections

Have you ever read love notes that seemed untrue? How do you know God's promises are trustworthy?

How would you contrast earthly love with God's eternal love? If you remember some favorite verses of promise, write them down.

2. *God is with us all the time (Zephaniah 3:17a).*

When we were dating, Snow came daily after work to sit on my front porch with my brother and me or watch television with my family. (He was always there at mealtime!) At night, Snow and I often sat on the front porch together. We talked for hours, asking all about each other—sharing our dreams and hopes for the future. We went everywhere together—to church, to movies, or out to dinner with friends and family.

As three years passed, I knew Snow loved me. I'd watched him sacrifice many things for my welfare, once rejecting a lucrative job in a distant city to stay near. I'd also depended on his promises in writing, as well as in action, many times. We planted a foundation for our future home together and were ready for marriage.

In Bible times, Jewish families accepted the tradition of arranged marriages, and young couples anticipated their traditional wedding surrounded by family. It was vitally important they marry within the Hebrew faith. Most married within a few miles of their homes, and—though they had little time together individually before the wedding—it's likely they knew each other from afar. Sometimes, as in the case of Rebekah (Genesis 24), new brides moved hundreds of miles to live with their new husbands and their families. After the wedding, they were constantly with each other, as brides left their families to live with their grooms. The young couple depended on each other and found intimacy as a bulwark against outside forces.

God is the most trustworthy loved one you have—standing near and giving you unending love. You can lean on His everlasting arms, as the hymn says, because He's always close, eager to listen. He's never away on business, never distracted, never too busy. The Old Testament prophet Zephaniah gives us this simple yet profound promise from our Bridegroom: *"The Lord your God is with you"* (3:17).

Chosen and Cherished

Love-Letter Bouquet

Read Isaiah 43:4–5. What does God tell you *not* to do, because He is with you?
Explain in your own words what comfort you gain from these words.

Why does God tell you not to be afraid?

Because you are _____.

Because He _____.

3. God is powerful enough to save you (Zephaniah 3:17b).

Snow was always my powerful protector and rescuer. Arriving home late one night, I got out of the car and walked toward the house when I realized the car was still moving—right toward a steep cliff near our back yard. I grabbed the door handle, trying to hold on, but I didn't have the physical strength to get in, press on the brake, and park the car safely. It continued to move slowly toward the cliff. Panicking, I called Snow, watching television in the living room in the front of the house. He heard my screams, ran out, pushed the car back, and parked it safely.

On another occasion, noises at the back door woke us in the middle of the night. Snow jumped out of bed, asked me to lock the bedroom door and stay there, then rushed toward the noise, where he frightened off a potential burglar with a baseball bat. I felt a sense of peace all during our marriage thanks to his courage and power.

In Old Testament times, husbands were known for their strength as warriors (2 Samuel 23:8–39) and would be expected to rescue their wives from any who meant to harm them (1 Samuel 30:18), Perhaps the average Hebrew husband even slept over the threshold to protect his family from wild animals or human intruders. Because he loved her, the bridegroom stood ever-ready to defend his bride. Women probably looked to their strong husbands as powerful protectors willing even to die for their family.

Yet, no matter how strong a bridegroom is—physically or spiritually, no one has the power to rescue and protect us like Almighty God. Zephaniah 3:17 states powerfully: *"He is mighty to save."* While the godly groom is a human reflection of Jesus, our all-powerful Defender and Savior, only our Lord Himself has the authority to save us from eternal damnation as a result of our sin.

Love-Letter Bouquet

Search the following verses and answer these questions:
- ❤ Psalm 31:1–5
- ❤ 2 Samuel 22:33–34
- ❤ Psalm 147:4–5
- ❤ Joshua 1:9
- ❤ Ephesians 1:18–21

What's the nature of God's power? How is that power shown in the life, death, and resurrection of Jesus?

If God's power is for us who believe, how do you think we should then live?

4. *God takes great delight in you (Zephaniah 3:17c).*

As a child, I couldn't believe that God, who created the whole world—hanging the sun, moon, and stars in place—took great delight in me, a skinny, mean, little kid. Then I discovered His love letters, especially these words in Zephaniah—His promise that He takes great delight in us.

The best grooms, whether in biblical times or today, take great pleasure in their wives. After all, few days are more joyous than the wedding day, the blissful uniting of a man and his beloved. But we as believers can look to Christ as the ideal Bridegroom, who has far more respect, love, and delight in us than any husband—or any other human—could give. He's able to bring us deep-down joy that will last for eternity.

Love-Letter Bouquet

Read Psalm 36:5–8. Write phrases about the excellence of God's love for you:

How do you know He loves you, just as you are?

Memorize Psalm 36:5–8 to keep close to your heart. Remind yourself to read these verses in times of trouble.

Read Ephesians 1:4 and 2:4–5. How has God shown His love in everyday life?

Can you remember times God showed His love when you needed it desperately? Explain:

5. God will quiet you with His love (Zephaniah 3:17∂).

When my husband died, a strange thing happened: I did not mourn—at all. The night he died, my children and I stood in a group hug and cried. After that, an amazing euphoria settled in my heart. I'd expected all the usual stages of grief: denial, anger, bitterness, and so forth. I kept waiting for the agony and gut-wrenching sorrow. It didn't come. At the funeral I sang hymns; when people expressed condolences, I felt a little ridiculous that I couldn't muster a tear! I later sought counseling since I was not experiencing any deep feeling. If I didn't express sorrow and get the anger out, would I crash and burn years later from pent-up emotions? No one offered a reason why I was so happy.

I searched my soul for answers. Since my husband died suddenly in the stadium at a high school football game, many of the crowd there dropped by my home after the game. Hundreds of them shook my hand, promising to pray for me. Could it be the prayer power was lifting me up, away from sadness? I looked for additional answers. My husband was a vibrant Christian, and he expected—and even anticipated—going to heaven. Could it be some of his joy, face-to-face with his Savior in heaven, was spilling down on me? Could it be in our covenant marriage I loved him to the extent that we really weren't two, but one flesh, one spirit? Could it be because my "better half" was already in heaven, that I had one foot in heaven already? I decided the correct answer was "all the above."

Then one day I found these few words from Zephaniah 3:17: *"(H)e will quiet you with His love."* Whatever the hurt, God had covered it. After years of questioning, I accepted the quiet, settled spirit within me. I knew this verse was true: God had quieted me with His overflowing love, and joy had come in the morning.

Love-Letter Bouquet

Read 1 Kings 19:11–12. Why do you think Elijah couldn't hear God's voice in the whirlwind but found it in His still, small voice?

Read Isaiah 32:17–18. What is the effect or result of righteousness in a person's life?

Read Isaiah 63:8–9, 14. Do you believe God is distressed when His people are distressed?

6. God will rejoice over you with singing (Zephaniah 3:17e).
When I first read this amazing verse, the words jumped off the page! Many times I had rejoiced over God by singing songs such as "Jesus Is the Sweetest Name I Know" or "Majesty," but it's unbelievable that our *Bridegroom* rejoices over *us* with singing. It was hard for me to realize He rejoices over us—*just as we are*. Now I'm convinced He looks down from heaven and says, "Look at that girl go! I sing over her, My church, My bride."

Here's incredible news: He loves you and me in a special way, no matter how often or how deeply we've sinned. Of course, as our Bridegroom, He also wants to protect us from anything that separates us from Him, drawing us back to His heart. No matter where we are spiritually, as long as we're His, *He sings* as He celebrates our lives, rejoicing over us daily!

A friend of mine in Clinton, Mississippi, said, "I've been reading Zephaniah 3. If God is singing over me, what's He singing?" Before I could answer, she belted out the 1960s song: "Bar-bar-bar Bar–bar–bra Ann, Bar-bar-bar Bar–bar–bra..."

"Stop," I said. "Somehow I can't see God singing that oldie over you. I don't know what He's singing. I just know He *is* singing over you because His Word says so. He sings His love songs to us all the time." I believe that truth with all my heart.

Love-Letter Bouquet

From Isaiah 43:1, 4, 10, list several reasons God may be rejoicing over you with singing:

According to Psalm 104:31, 34, do you think God expects reciprocal joy and singing from you, His creation?

Spend time today praising Him and welcome His love and acceptance.

A DEEPER WALK WITH YOUR GROOM

As you walk with Christ to complete this study, ask Him to draw you to His heart as you yearn for His presence. Pray that He will change you, helping you know Him better as you take a deeper walk through the following Scriptures:

- 💜 Deuteronomy 31:6, 8
- 💜 Hebrews 13:5–6
- 💜 Deuteronomy 4:29, 31; 26:18; 30:20
- 💜 Isaiah 60:1
- 💜 Isaiah 58:11, 14
- 💜 Philippians 4:4, 13

How has God encouraged you through these verses?

PRAYER

All-powerful God, help me to be quiet before You, lean on You for strength, and face the future with confidence. I trust You'll never leave me; I know You love me and take delight in me, even though I don't deserve Your great, pure love. I praise You, O Lord, and bow before You as your chosen and cherished bride. Amen.

INSIGHTS

KETUBAH

The marriage covenant, or *ketubah*, is still a sacred religious and legal document for many twenty-first-century Jewish couples. The version generally used today was written by Simeon ben Shetach in 80 B.C. and is in Aramaic, the language used by the Jews of that day (and the language Jesus eventually would speak). The document is meant to outline the basic responsibilities of the husband to his wife (essentially protecting the wife's rights). After signing the ketubah, along with two witnesses, the groom presents it to his bride at the wedding ceremony (in modern custom). In many contemporary Jewish families, the ketubah is ornately decorated, framed, and placed on a prominent wall in the home as a reminder of God's blessing on the marriage and family.

Source: http://judaism.about.com/cs/jewishweddings/f/ketubah.htm

PRAYER & PRAISE
JOURNAL

CHAPTER THREE

BOUGHT WITH A PRICE

By Joy Brown

The concept of the bride-price is somewhat foreign to the Western mind-set. However, not only was it a part of the biblical wedding, it is still a common cultural practice in some regions of the world today. It provides us a beautiful portrait of the cost our Bridegroom paid so He could live in relationship with us.

The bridegroom paid the bride's father (and in later times the entire family) the bride-price in order to marry his daughter. In an agrarian society, it was meant to compensate for the loss of her labor in the fields and also the work she would have done in her family, such as homemaking chores, handiwork, or other duties.

The bride-price is different from a *dowry*. A dowry is paid by the family of the bride to the groom (or sometimes the family of the groom) to establish the new household. The bride-price is also different from a *dower*. A dower is a gift the groom gives to his bride, often on the day of the wedding.

Previously, we looked at the contract/covenant, or *ketubah*, the bridegroom presented before the betrothal. The bride-price was stated in the *ketubah*, and it was commensurate with the social status of the bridegroom. He gave the dearest things he could afford—land, money, livestock, or jewels. He could also give *bride service*, especially if he were not wealthy enough to pay a large bride price.

A perfect example of bride service is found in Genesis 29:14–30. Jacob gave seven years of service to Laban in order to marry his younger daughter, Rachel. Laban deceived Jacob and gave Leah to him as his wife since it was the custom that the oldest daughter should marry first. (She evidentially was veiled at the wedding, so Jacob did not know his bride was Leah.) When the deception was revealed, Jacob married Rachel a week later, but had to work for Laban another seven years to fulfill the bride-price for Rachel.

Some people consider the bride-price to be degrading to women, stating that the groom is buying the bride. However, since the biblical betrothal was legally binding and the couple was accepting each other's liabilities and assets, in many ways it was a protection. Should the bridegroom die during the betrothal, the bride-price would be passed to the bride so that she would have financial support after his death.

Ruined?

Our older daughter, Meri Beth, was to be married on a Saturday at five o'clock in the evening. On that Thursday afternoon, our house was filled with out-of-town family and friends who had arrived early for the wedding. The kitchen was overflowing with food and laughter as the guests sat around talking and eating.

The phone rang and I heard the shocking words, "Mrs. Brown, this is the dry cleaners. I don't know how to tell you this, but we have ruined your daughter's wedding dress. Instead of steaming the white velvet dress, our worker brought the pressing head down on it and it's ruined. This is the worst mistake we've ever made in 35 years of business."

My husband, Wayne, got the dress from the cleaners, and we found that the words were not exaggerated. Indeed, the dress had been ruined.

What happened? Well, you'll find a valuable lesson in how it turned out if you can wait until the end of the chapter....

Right now I want you to think about how you are entering this study. Do you feel that you, like Meri Beth's wedding dress, are ruined? Do you feel far from God? Do you feel hopeless? If so, please study this chapter carefully. If not, please be in prayer for those who are experiencing those feelings as you study. Remember, you are chosen and cherished, and your Bridegroom loves you with an everlasting love!

THE PRICE OUR BRIDEGROOM PAID

Our Bridegroom paid the ultimate bride-price. He gave His life's blood for His bride: *"Be shepherds of the church of God, which he bought with his own blood"* (Acts 20:28). It seems that in today's society there is less emphasis on the blood of Jesus than in past generations. Some people refer to Christianity as a "bloody religion" or "slaughterhouse religion." Certain denominations have even removed all songs that speak of the blood of Jesus.

I recently went to two large Christian bookstores trying to find resources on the blood of Jesus. I was shocked to find only one book on the subject in these large stores. The devaluing of the blood of Jesus is sad, for we are told in Scripture that *"without the shedding of blood there is no forgiveness"* (Hebrews 9:22).

Why is the blood of Jesus so important? The remainder of this chapter will deal with that question. However, from the outset we need to establish the fact that the "blood of Jesus" is representative of His death. In Leviticus 17:11 we read, *"For the life of a creature is in the blood, and I have given it to you to make atonement for yourselves on the altar; it is the blood that makes atonement for one's life."* His blood (and thus His death) makes atonement for our sin.

THE CONCEPT OF ATONEMENT IN THE OLD TESTAMENT

According to Abingdon's *Strong's Exhaustive Concordance of the Bible*, the Hebrew word for "atonement" is *kaphar*, which means "to cover." Figuratively, it means, among other things, "to expiate, to placate or cancel."

Jesus' sacrificial death of atonement was foreshadowed in the Old Testament. Even though there were sacrifices of cereals and liquids (mostly wine), the four types of sacrifices that receive the most consideration in the New Testament teachings are those associated with animal sacrifices: burnt offering, peace offering, sin offering, and guilt offering. Since Jesus's first followers were Jewish, the concept of a sacrificial death should have been familiar to them, for throughout their lives they had presented sacrifices for atonement of their sins.

With each of the four sacrifices, the worshipper drew near the altar with the animal he proposed to offer as a sign of preparation for worship. He laid his hand on the head of the animal, indicating that he was identifying with the sacrifice. As he did so, he confessed his sins. According to Leon Morris's book *The Atonement*, some scholars believe this was a symbolic act of transference of sin to the animal that would be slain.

The worshipper then killed the animal as atonement for his sins. Then the blood of the animal was collected and the priest used it as was fitting for the offering. Sometimes it was sprinkled on the altar, the curtain, or the people. Other times it was poured out at the base of the altar. See the Book of Leviticus 1–7.

Part of the animal was burned on the altar as *an aroma pleasing to the Lord* (Leviticus 1:9, 13, 19). The rest of the carcass was disposed of, sometimes being given to the priests for food (Leviticus 7:8).

God's nature requires that sin be punished. Isaiah 59:2 states, *"But your iniquities have separated you from your God; your sins have hidden his face from you, so that he will not hear."* As we will learn below, God's wrath is poured out on sin, because it separates Him from humankind.

Love-Letter Bouquet

Read the following Scriptures and write down the name(s) of the person(s) who offered animal sacrifices to God and why they did so:
- ♥ Genesis 4:1–7
- ♥ Genesis 8:18–22
- ♥ Genesis 22:1–14
- ♥ Exodus 12:1–13
- ♥ Exodus 24:1–8
- ♥ 2 Chronicles 7:1–6
- ♥ Luke 2:22–24

As you read the following Scriptures, underline the positive words that describe our God.

"The Lord is slow to anger, abounding in love and forgiving sin and rebellion. Yet he does not leave the guilty unpunished."
—Numbers 14:18

Chosen and Cherished

"The LORD, the LORD, the compassionate and gracious God, slow to anger, abounding in love and faithfulness, maintaining love to thousands, and forgiving wickedness, rebellion and sin. Yet he does not leave the guilty unpunished; he punishes the children and their children for the sin of the fathers to the third and fourth generation."
—Exodus 34:6–7

"The LORD is slow to anger and great in power; the Lord will not leave the guilty unpunished."
—Nahum 1:3

"Have nothing to do with a false charge and do not put an innocent or honest to death, for I will not acquit the guilty."
—Exodus 23:7

Now, go back to these four verses and place two lines under the phrases that express God's response to sin.

Note: Elsewhere in the Bible, it is clear that each person is responsible before God for his or her own sin (see Ezekiel 18:14–20). As Beth Moore points out in her study *Breaking Free*, the Hebrew word used in Exodus 34:7 for "punishes" is *paqad*, which means "to count, number." God does not punish our children for our sin, but rather He is aware of how the consequences of our sin affect future generations.

Do you see the pattern here? Because God is just, honest, loving, forgiving, compassionate, gracious, faithful, and powerful (and righteous) He cannot allow sin to go unpunished. The Hebrew word for "unpunished" is *naqah*, which it means "to be (or to make) clean." God's nature requires punishment for sin. We cannot cleanse ourselves of our sins. So He provided the way. He took on Himself the punishment for our sin. He paid the bride-price with His own blood, redeeming us so we could live in relationship with Him.

A careful study of Jesus's death reveals that all the requirements of the sacrificial system set forth in the Torah (the first five books of the Bible) were met. I would like to encourage you to examine the fascinating correlations. However, for this study we will only look at three crucial aspects of Jesus's death, each of which is central to its sacrificial nature.

Jesus is a man. He dealt with sin in the same nature where it occurred. Hebrews 2:14–17 clearly defines this fact. *"For this reason he had to be made like his brothers in every way, in order that he might become a merciful and faithful high priest in service to God, and that he might make atonement for the sins of the people"* (Hebrews 2:17).

Reflections

God became human so He could die for your sins. Write down three adjectives to describe your feelings about that fact.

Jesus is sinless and holy. The sacrificial animals were to be without spot or blemish (Exodus 12:5). Jesus was *"holy, blameless, pure, set apart from sinners, exalted above the heavens. Unlike the other high priests, he does not need to offer sacrifices day after day, first for his own sins, and then for the sins of the people. He sacrificed for their sins once for all when he offered himself"* (Hebrews 7:26–27).

Love-Letter Bouquet

Read 1 Peter 1:19 and Hebrews 9:14. In the space below, reflect on Jesus's nature and character. Think of ways He showed that He was blameless and pure even while facing temptation and/or opposition.

Jesus is God. As we have seen, Jesus took on the form of a man so that He could deal with sin in the same nature where it occurred—humanity. However, Jesus also is God.

Only God can forgive sin: *"Who can forgive sins but God alone?"* (Mark 2:7). A study of the deity of Christ is a rich and rewarding experience. However, for the purposes set forth in this chapter, we will look at only a few proofs. May these Scriptures fill you with wonder as you realize that the God of the universe, Jesus Christ, paid the bride-price so you could be His bride!

Love-Letter Bouquet

Read and savor the following Scriptures that show Jesus's divinity.

- ♥ Jesus is "God with us" (Isaiah 7:14; Matthew 1:23).
- ♥ The Word was made flesh (John 1:14).
- ♥ Jesus was in nature God but became a man (1 Timothy 3:16; Philippians 2:6–7).
- ♥ Jesus is the image of God (Colossians 1:15–20).
- ♥ In Jesus, the fullness of the Deity lives in bodily form (Colossians 2:9)
- ♥ Jesus declared, "I and the Father are one" (John 10:30).
- ♥ Salvation is found in no one else except Jesus (Acts 4:12).

POWER IN THE BLOOD

The sacrificial blood of Jesus *atones* for our sins. Scripture describes the benefits and effects of the power of His blood in a number of other ways as well: the blood of Jesus offers forgiveness (Ephesians 1:7); redemption (1 Peter 1:18); salvation from God's wrath (Romans 5:9); purification (cleansing) from sin (1 John 1:7); propitiation or satisfaction of the death penalty sin merits (Romans 3:25); freedom from the curse of sin (Galatians 3:13); justification/righteousness (Romans 3:23–24); access to God (Ephesians 2:13; Hebrews 10:19); reconciliation with God (Colossians 1:20; 2 Corinthians 5:17–19); protection (Exodus 12:13); and victorious power (Revelation 12:10–11).

Take a moment to review each of these benefits. Can you think of anything you could possibly need in life that is not covered by the blood of Jesus?

His blood brought us life and an intimate relationship with Him as our loving Bridegroom.

Love-Letter Bouquet

Please take time to read the Scriptures listed above. Meditate on how the blood of Jesus affects your life. Underline in your Bible the benefits that mean the most to you and tell why they are important in your life.

COVENANTS IN SCRIPTURE

Covenants made throughout the Bible were solemn promises not to be broken. In a covenant relationship, each partner took on both the liabilities and assets of the other, and a sacrifice was made to seal the deal and signify its importance. In Genesis 15, God made a unilateral covenant with Abraham, which sets the foundation for the rest of the Old Testament.

In Jeremiah 31:31–37 God promised to make a new covenant with Israel and Judah. He said *"I will put my law in their minds and write it on their hearts"* (v. 33) and *"I will forgive their wickedness and will remember their sins no more"* (v. 34).

Jesus is the mediator of that new covenant (Hebrews 12:24). He told His disciples the night before He was crucified, *"This is my blood of the covenant, which is poured out for many for the forgiveness of sins"* (Matthew 26:27).

When our Bridegroom paid the bride-price, He sealed the new covenant. Sacrificial animals are no longer needed to atone for our sins: *"But when this priest offered for all time one sacrifice for sins, he sat down at the right hand of God"* (Hebrews 10:12).

THE REST OF THE STORY

Still wondering about my daughter's wedding dress fiasco? I took the ruined dress to the seamstress, Sarah Marsh, who had made the beautiful, personally designed dress. Sarah immediately began ripping it apart. My husband, Wayne, called for material to be flown in overnight from the place we had purchased it. Sarah worked nonstop Friday and Saturday.

The first chance Meri Beth had to try on the newly fashioned dress was right before she walked down the aisle. It was as beautiful as the original dress and was an even better fit.

May this story be a reminder that your Bridegroom has removed the sin and ruin in your life. Because He loves you, He bought you at great price. He makes all things new, even better than before! Hallelujah, what a Savior!

PRAYER

Dear Lord, thank You for being the God of the sacrificial bride-price and of new beginnings. In Jesus's name, amen.

INSIGHTS

UNBROKEN UNION

Though the bride-price is not a part of contemporary Jewish wedding custom, the wedding ring serves a similar purpose. Traditionally, there is only one ring, the one the groom presents to his bride. It must be worth at least one *perutah*, a small coin used in ancient times.

The ring represents the formal bond of the marriage. By giving the ring, the groom acquires exclusive rights to the bride's hand in marriage. Thus, no other man can be intimate with her.

Jewish tradition holds that the ring should be an unadorned band of pure gold, free of precious stones and even inscriptions. A simple, unpierced band is symbolic of wholeness and the unbroken union marriage represents. My heart is filled with wonder as I realize that I have entered into an unbroken union with Jesus Christ!

Source: http://www.chabad.org/library/article_cdo/aid/477319/jewish/
Is-a-Double-Ring-wedding-ceremony-okay.htm

PRAYER & PRAISE
JOURNAL

Chapter Four

A Choice of Cups

By Joy Brown

My husband, Wayne, proposed to me when he was in seminary and I was in college. On Easter Sunday night, after we had attended a worship service and gone out to eat, we went back to my parents' home. The house was quiet that night as my family members were already in bed asleep. Wayne had planned for the two of us to have a private Communion service reflecting on God's atoning love.

As we knelt around the coffee table in the living room, we offered each other the bread and the cup. When we finished with a prayer, Wayne nervously handed me a beautifully wrapped gift. He explained, "I started to give this to you last night so you could wear it with your Easter dress today, but I decided to wait until Easter Sunday."

From his comment, I thought I would see a broach. However, inside the package was a beautiful engagement ring. I immediately looked at Wayne and asked, "But what about the butterfly?' (Wayne laughs today and says that is not the response he expected.)

"What butterfly?" he replied, completely baffled.

I reminded him of a comment he had made years before we started dating. A group of our teenaged friends were gathered at the local drive-in restaurant, laughing and talking while sitting on the hoods of our cars. The topic of conversation that night was a young couple who had just become engaged. Wayne made the statement, "To me that's like taking a little butterfly and clipping its wings." I remember looking at him and thinking, "That boy will never marry."

After I helped him recall the statement, he smiled and said, "That was before I fell in love with you."

Then he got on one knee and asked, "Will you marry me?"

I happily accepted. After it was sealed with a kiss, we looked at each other and said, "What are we supposed to do next?" We decided that telling my parents was the appropriate course of action.

Tiptoeing to my parents' bedroom, I awakened them and showed them the ring. They followed me back down the hall, with my father—who had a good sense of humor—carrying his shotgun! Then we celebrated and sat down to make some preliminary wedding plans. We still tease my mother about her being so excited that she finished the rest of the grape juice from our Communion.

THE MOMENT OF DECISION

In the wedding custom of the biblical period, after the marriage contract had been read in the presence of at least two witnesses, and after the bridal gift(s) was given, the future bride had a choice to accept or reject the proposal. She would confer with her father to see if he agreed with her decision. Then, the bridegroom would pour a cup of wine and drink half of it. If the future bride accepted his proposal, she would drink the other half. If not, she would decline.

If she accepted, the couple was officially, legally married. However, they could not be in each other's presence until after the wedding ceremony. From that day on, each time the bride went into public she wore a veil to show that she was betrothed, "set apart" for her bridegroom.

This physical example has deep spiritual truth. We've been chosen by and for our Bridegroom, Jesus Christ. His written contract is filled with beautiful promises He offers to us. He gave His life's blood as our bridal price. Now we, like the bride of Bible times, must make a decision. Do we accept His proposal and let others know that we are "set apart" for Him, or do we walk away from the cup in refusal?

Chosen and Cherished

OUR SAVIOR'S CUP

The cup is one of the Bible's richest symbols. It is a Jewish idiom for an experience that completely engulfs you. It can be an experience either of joy or affliction.

As previously mentioned, the couple drank from a common cup to seal the betrothal. The next time they would do so would come at the end of the actual wedding ceremony. That cup would represent full and complete joy.

When I began to look at various Scriptures referring to *the cup*, two types of experiences became evident to me: the cup of affliction and the cup of joy. And I realized that, symbolically, Jesus drank all the cups of affliction as our Bridegroom and offers us, as His bride, all the cups of joy.

His was a bitter cup indeed. The sinless Son of God knew that by drinking the cup He would bear the sins of all mankind, for He is *"the Lamb of God who takes away the sin of the world"* (John 1:29). He struggled in Gethsemane with whether or not there could be another way to purchase His beloved bride. Since there was no other way, He willingly surrendered and accepted the bitter cup set before Him.

Love-Letter Bouquet

Read Luke 22:39–44. As you read of the agony of Jesus on your behalf, how does it make you feel? Write your responses in the space below.

Read Numbers 5:11–31. (As used here, the word *thigh* is a euphemism for the womb.) Also, read Hosea 1:1–2. We are *"guilty of the vilest adultery in departing from the Lord"* (v. 2). How do these verses affect your view of your own sin?

Our Bridegroom drank the bitter cup for us. As a result, He experienced *"bitter suffering"* (Numbers 5:24, 27) and died. He accepted the curse of sin (Galatians 3:13) so we could be declared innocent! There are four important aspects of the cup Jesus drank on our behalf:

1. His cup contained the fury of God's wrath. God hates sin. Jesus accepted the punishment for our sins by His death on the Cross. In fact, 2 Corinthians 5:21 states: *"God made him who had no sin to be sin for us, so that in him we might become the righteousness of God."*

Sin always carries with it a curse. When Jesus died on the Cross, He symbolically drank of the cup of God's fury *"becoming a curse for us, for it is written, 'Cursed is everyone who is hung on a tree'"* (Galatians 3:13).

Love-Letter Bouquet

Read Ephesians 2:1–10. We were by nature children of wrath, deserving of death and hell. But, out of his great love, Jesus took our place and made us alive in Him. Give thanks for his mercies!

2. *His cup contained scorn and derision.* We read of the cup of scorn and derision in Ezekiel 23:32. The Romans considered crucifixion to be so shameful that they wouldn't allow their own citizens to undergo this form of capital punishment. One of the goals of crucifixion was to publicly humiliate and disgrace the offender. Imagine being stripped of clothing, being tortured, screaming in agony, dying as people stood watching, wagering on your clothing or the length of time it would take for you to die.... This is a picture of the scorn and derision your Bridegroom endured on your behalf.

In addition, *"those who passed by hurled insults at Him...shaking their heads"* (Mark 15:29) to reinforce their mockery. As Ernest L. Martin writes in *Secrets of Golgotha*, some Bible scholars believe Jesus may have been pelted with stones as well. The religious charge against Him was blasphemy, because He told them that He was God. Before the Jewish people came under Roman occupation, the capital punishment for blasphemy was stoning and then hanging the dead body on a tree. They couldn't stone Him to death, but they probably were allowed to throw some stones according to their custom.

Love-Letter Bouquet

Read Hebrews 12:2. Do you realize that *you*—as part of His church, His redeemed bride—are the joy set before Him?

Reflections

Take a few moments to repeat aloud the words, "I am His joy." In the space below, share your feelings about this statement.

3. His cup contained ruin and desolation. Sin always brings destruction. Jesus said, *"'The thief* [sin/Satan] *comes only to steal and kill and destroy; I have come that they may have life and have it to the full'"* (John 10:10, author's words in brackets).

At His death, Jesus drank from the cup of ruin and desolation so *we* would not have to do so. Yet, we're prone to choose the things in life that will pull us from Him rather than to Him. These will eventually bring some sort of destruction to our lives.

Some wrong choices bring emotional destruction, others spiritual destruction, others physical destruction. The Bible offers Moses as an example of right choices: *"He chose to be mistreated along with the people of God rather than to enjoy the pleasures of sin for a season"* (Hebrews 11:25).

Love-Letter Bouquet

What correlations do you see between the pleasures of sin and ruin and desolation? (John 10:10 and Hebrews 11:25)

Consider the sin to which you are most prone. List ways that sin could lead to ruin and desolation in your life or in the life of another.

Reflections

Whisper a prayer of praise to your Bridegroom for providing victory over sin and for sparing you from its ruin and desolation.

4. His cup contained trembling and death. In Gethsemane Jesus told His disciples, *"My soul is overwhelmed with sorrow to the point of death. Stay here and keep watch with me'"* (Matthew 26:38). This verse breaks my heart. I can hardly bear to think of my Bridegroom in such agony over paying the price for my sin.

When Jesus died on the Cross, He paid the penalty for *our* sinful condition so we wouldn't have to face the judgment sin requires. When God forgives our sins, He doesn't just excuse them. Christ bore the punishment in our place!

I wanted to convey the depth of this glorious truth to the teenagers I was leading during a youth conference in the beautiful mountains of North Carolina. I had enjoyed a marvelous week with them, and we had become so close they nicknamed me "Ma." Aided by two of the boys in the group, I devised a plan to try to teach the beauty of Christ's substitutionary death.

In class the next day, John (the class clown) stood up in the middle of Bible Study and hollered, "Ma, this is boring! Let's do something else!" Then he fell to the floor. I turned to John and, pretending to lose my cool, demanded that he go back to his cottage and confess his rude behavior to his chaperones. The class sat in stunned silence, partly because of John's behavior and partly because they had never seen me angry. "Go now!" I demanded.

John turned sadly and began walking toward the door as his best friend, Ray, stood up and said, "No, Ma. Please don't make him go. He's already in trouble with the chaperones, and if he goes back they will send him home. I'll go in his place."

"No," I replied, seemingly angry. "John did this and John must pay for his actions."

"Please, Ma, I want to do this for my best friend," Ray said as he turned and quietly walked out the door.

I turned to the stunned teenagers and said, "This is exactly what Jesus Christ did for you." (Later I was thrilled to see many of the teenagers accept Christ as their Savior during the commitment time.)

Love-Letter Bouquet

Read 1 Peter 2:24: *"By his wounds you have been healed."* Please personalize that glorious truth and repeat the phrase seven times slowly as you let its beauty permeate your heart.

OUR CUP

We've looked at the cup of afflictions Jesus drank in our place. By contrast, our portion of the cup of acceptance is filled with the blessings our Bridegroom makes available to us. Through His sacrificial death, we drink the cup of *salvation* (Psalm 116:13), the cup of *consolation* (Jeremiah 16:7), and the cup of *blessing* (1 Corinthians 10:16 KJV).

Yes, our Bridegroom drank the bitterness of the cup so we could drink the blessings of the cup. Everything our Bridegroom did and continues to do is to show His love for His bride. No other Bridegroom has so loved His bride!

Accepting God's Proposal

How do we respond to His love? How do we become betrothed to this wonderful Bridegroom?

We recognize and admit our sinful condition and the fact that we cannot take away our own sin. We cannot pay our debt, the penalty of sinning against Holy God. We are all God's creation, but we are *not* all His bride. Only those who choose to enter into relationship with Him are His bride.

To become His bride, we accept in faith what our Bridegroom did for us on the Cross, when He took the punishment for our sinfulness. He bore our sins and gave His life's blood to buy us back from the sinful state we were in. In response, we acknowledge His gift and commit to live in relationship with Him, the Risen Lord, forever.

When we do, through a miracle of the Holy Spirit, He enters our lives and we are forever joined with Him in a holy relationship. Our goal for the rest of our lives is to become more like our wonderful Bridegroom. Then one day, we will see our Bridegroom face-to-face and live with Him eternally in the home He is now preparing for us.

This relationship is possible only because He drank from the bitter cup and offers us the cup of joy. Will you accept it?

PRAYER

Dear Lord, Your love for me is so amazing I have no words to adequately express my response. I simply say, "I love you, too." In Jesus's name I pray, amen.

INSIGHTS

THE CUP WE SHARE

While savoring the meaning of the cup of acceptance,
I wrote the following poem. I pray it will be a blessing
to you:

The Cup that we share is far from the same;
　　mine smells of joy while His reeks of shame.
My portion is wholesome but His so much worse;
　　for mine is a blessing and His is a curse.
The cup shows God's love, its depth and its breadth.
My part brings new life while His brought cruel death.
And so, as our lips touch the cup in a pledge,
　　I taste the sweet fruit while He drinks the dregs.

Chosen and Cherished

PRAYER & PRAISE
JOURNAL

CHAPTER FIVE

SHOWERED WITH GIFTS

By Edna Ellison

After we had dated for several years, my boyfriend Snow kneeled and asked me to marry him. He was a great Christian young man, and I loved him very much. Of course I said yes. He then asked me to shop with him for an engagement ring. We selected a sparkling diamond in a beautiful setting.

After I showed my parents and friends the ring, several unexpected people asked if they could give me bridal showers: a new friend, a longtime friend with whom I had grown up, and an extended family member who wanted to give a family-couples shower. I helped them form guest lists, and the fun began! I began to realize most friends and families hold a bride in esteem she doesn't deserve. I learned traditions I'd never heard of, such as seating the bride in a throne-like chair, giving her a corsage, and assigning others as her assistants. These "ladies-in-waiting" would list in a special notebook the gift givers' names, describe each gift in detail, and collect addresses for thank-you notes to be mailed—at the latest—two weeks after the wedding. (Some of them came to my home and helped write, address, and stamp them.) I got ten sets of sheets, a full set of dishes in my chosen china pattern, and many other useful small appliances and items for our home. The parties and gifts were an unforgettable part of our marriage experience!

GIFTS OF PREPARATION

Marriage traditions vary worldwide, but usually a central theme in all cultures is the giving of gifts to brides. To one degree or another, twenty-first-century families and friends still maintain gift-giving traditions begun in ancient times. In Bible days, when the groom's father had chosen a bride for his son, both his family and the bride's own family gave her gifts. The groom's father gave gifts to her family to compensate for their daughter's departure to marry his son; he also gave her garments, oils, and beauty products for her beautification and purification before the ceremony, and joined her own family in giving gifts to her to decorate the bridal chamber (after the marriage ceremony) and make it a comfortable place to live.

For centuries Jewish brides have engaged in a ritual bath, called *mikvah*, in a free-flowing stream of "living water," before their wedding ceremonies. Sometimes women in the family accompany them as they immerse two or three times and repeat a blessing; it is a special time of spiritual rather than physical cleansing (though it is practiced after their monthly cycle).

Love-Letter Bouquet

Read Genesis 24:52 and circle below the way Abraham gave gifts to Isaac's future wife, Rebekah.
- Through personal contact with Rebekah's father.
- Through a servant.
- Through a mother's arrangement.

Read verses 59–66. Who went, perhaps as witnesses or chaperones, with Rebekah to meet Isaac?

Read Proverbs 18:16. Do you think it's easy to be impressed by the groom's ring or extravagant gifts, rather than a God-led and God-blessed union in holy matrimony?

Read Isaiah 1:23, 28. What happened to the leaders who "chase after gifts"?

Sometimes marriages move in a direction away from God and toward material possessions. How have you seen that misdirection in your marriage or among people you know? Explain.

Can a bride-to-be focus on the shower, gifts from the groom, and the management of other gifts so much that she and her groom are starting their marriage with the wrong focus? How can she change the direction of her engagement period and prepare properly for a long, godly marriage "for better or worse, till death do us part"?

In your church, how can you encourage church members not to be greedy? How can you encourage them not to be overly concerned with the church's material possessions?

GENERAL GIFTS: LIFE, SALVATION, AND THE SPIRIT

Of course, everything in life on earth is a gift of our Father God: air, water, food, family—any good thing in the universe. We couldn't list all God's physical gifts in this book. Paul tells the church at Ephesus a miraculous fact: salvation is a gift. *"For it is by grace you have been saved, through faith—and this not from yourselves, it is the gift of God"* (Ephesians 2:8).

John gives us the account of Jesus and the Samaritan woman at Jacob's well, in which He said, *"'If you knew the gift of God and who it is that asks you for a drink, you would have asked him and he would have given you living water'"* (John 4:10). He explains that the *gift* of living water He offers will *"become in you a spring of water welling up to eternal life"* (v. 14).

Luke also records a speech Peter made to a crowd in Jerusalem describing the incredible, supernatural gift of the Holy Spirit: *"Peter replied, 'Repent and be baptized, every one of you, in the name of Jesus Christ for the forgiveness of your sins. And you will receive the gift of the Holy Spirit'"* (Acts 2:38). After Pentecost, Jewish believers accepted God's gifts, and finally came to realize that even Gentiles could receive God's Holy Spirit in their hearts (Acts 10:45).

Through Christ you and I possess more gifts than we can name: *"every spiritual blessing in Christ"* (Ephesians 1:3): faith, hope, joy, grace, wisdom, understanding, godly strength, endurance, patience, thanksgiving, redemption, and forgiveness of sins (Colossians 1:3–13). In fact, the mystery for all of us is that gifts beyond naming or counting are found in Christ, *"in whom are hidden all the treasures."* (Colossians 2:3). James 1:17 puts it plainly: *"Every good and perfect gift is from above, coming down from the Father."*

Love-Letter Bouquet

Read Matthew 7:11. What is the most extravagant gift you have given one of your children?

How often do you tell your children of the gifts God gives us every day?

How can you tell others about the source of your gifts?

Are you thankful for your Bridegroom, not just His gifts?

GIFTS OF ENCOURAGEMENT

In Romans 1:11–12, Paul gives an example of Christians encouraging one another with spiritual gifts. He says, *"I long to see you so that I may impart to you some spiritual gift to make you strong — that is, that you and I may be mutually encouraged by each other's faith."*

God didn't intend for Christians to live in an isolated world. The church, His bride, is a wonderful institution designed especially for the encouragement of all Christians in fellowship with each other.

God tells us that each one of us is given at least one spiritual gift at the time of salvation. It's up to us to use that gift in the kingdom of God. Once, through study and prayer (often with others), you diagnose which spiritual gifts God has given you, you can begin, in God's strength, to exercise your gifts in your church and in the world outside it. What joy to be a channel of God as He builds the church, His bride, and moves through your spirit to show His love!

Paul shares this list of spiritual gifts with the church in Rome — prophesying, serving, teaching, encouraging, contributing to the needs of others, leadership, showing mercy (Romans 12:6–8). Paul also writes these words to the church at Corinth:

> *Now about spiritual gifts, brothers, I do not want you to be ignorant.... There are different kinds of gifts, but the same Spirit. There are different kinds of service, but the same Lord. There are different kinds of working, but the same God works all of them in all men. Now to each one the manifestation of the Spirit is given for the common good.*
> —1 Corinthians 12:1, 4–7

Then he lists the following gifts: the message of wisdom, the message of knowledge, faith, gifts of healing, miraculous powers, prophecy, distinguishing between spirits, speaking in different kinds of tongues, and interpretations of tongues. Paul makes it clear that the Spirit *"gives them to each one, just as he determines"* (v. 11). Later he lists other gifts, some of which overlap: apostles, prophets, teachers, workers of miracles, those having gifts of healing, and those speaking in different kinds of tongues (v. 28).

What an amazing Bridegroom we have to give us such a diversity of gifts!

Love-Letter Bouquet

Choose several gifts above and write how they could be used in your church for the good of the congregation, the bride of Christ.

Read 1 Corinthians 12:12–27. Which part of the body do you think you are?

What does this passage in 1 Corinthians mean for you as one flesh with your earthly husband? How about your relationships with other church members? Are there some who are hard to accept?

Reflections

Which spiritual gift(s) do you think you have? Do you have a passion for one or several of these areas? Which ones? Pray, asking God to confirm these likely gifts.

Often someone else can identify our gifts better than we can. Ask a friend to tell you which gifts she thinks you have.

How could God be calling you to use even more of your gift as the bride of Christ?

Let us, His church and His bride, pray for the unity of His people as we serve Him with our various gifts.

THANKFUL FOR HIS GIFTS

As a child, I didn't understand why I should give God a dime of every dollar in my allowance. A nickel seemed adequate, and besides, it was larger, and made a louder sound in the collection plate. My parents wanted me to *save* another dime of my allowance, and that step left me with only 80 cents on the dollar! I sometimes hid my money or claimed I lost my tithe.

I was not a Christian then, and God had not softened my heart. After I asked Jesus into my heart a few years later, I cheerfully gave much more, not because I believed it helped me earn my way to heaven, but because I finally realized God owned everything. Money, other material possessions, and life itself. What a difference salvation makes! When He owns our hearts, He gives us a generous, thankful spirit that comes from the Holy Spirit. We realize the greatest gift He's given us is Himself, which frees us to act out of love and gratitude.

Love-Letter Bouquet

Read Ecclesiastes 5:19 and decide ways you can show you're grateful for God's physical and spiritual gifts.

In 1 Timothy 4:13–16, Paul warns his young minister/helper not to neglect his spiritual gifts. Which ones does he name? Which gifts do you think God wants you to use and grow?

Romans 11:29 tells us God's gifts and His call are irrevocable. What does that mean to you as an active Christian?

In which three ways does Romans 12:8 tell us to use the gifts of giving, leading, and showing mercy?

Read Hebrews 10:22–24. How are you preparing as you await Jesus's gift of final purification in heaven? Praise Him for intimacy in His cleansing power over body and soul.

PRAYER

Father, thank You for all the gifts you've given me. I love You, Lord, and want to use Your gifts generously, diligently, and cheerfully. Help me seek purity, build up the church, encourage others, and serve You in my world. Amen.

INSIGHTS

HARD-TO-FORGET GIFT

Many brides and grooms have a good story about an unusual wedding gift. My daughter Patsy and son-in-law Tim are among them.

My mother, Mary Martin, loved to shop for bargains. After my father died, as the matriarch over a substantial number of family members, she still loved giving abundant gifts. At Christmastime, she exchanged gifts with every child, grandchild, and great-grandchild. The year Patsy and Tim got married, after mother had already selected expensive Christmas sweaters for all the granddaughters (on sale, of course!), she saw a beautiful array of bedding sets for all sizes of beds. She decided the sale was just too good a bargain to skip.

At the family Christmas celebration, Patsy got a beautiful sweater. She turned to show it to Tim, and then she asked him what he got.

"I got pink sheets with roses and bows." He raised his eyebrows. "Do you think she meant to give these to *you*?"

"No," Patsy answered, smiling. "I don't think you'd want this sweater. You can sleep on these sheets, can't you?"

Then they both burst out laughing. It was a unique gift, the first pink sheets with roses and bows Tim had ever received, and a gift he would never forget.

Chosen and Cherished

PRAYER & PRAISE
JOURNAL

CHAPTER SIX

WATCHING AND WAITING

By Joy Brown

*I*n Bible times, the father of the groom supervised the construction of the wedding chamber. He alone made the decision as to when the bridal chamber had been adequately prepared for the bride. In fact, when a Jewish young man was asked when his wedding would take place, he may have replied along these lines, "Of that day or hour no man knows but my father only."

THE WEDDING DATE

When the father determined the bridal chamber was ready, he told his son to go get his bride for the wedding ceremony. Usually this occurred at midnight a year or so after the betrothal.

The bridegroom immediately alerted a good friend (comparable to a "best man" in today's culture) who blew the shofar and ran through the streets announcing that the wedding ceremony was about to take place. *"At midnight the cry rang out: 'Here's the bridegroom! Come out to meet him'"* (Matthew 25:6).

Likewise, only God knows exactly when Jesus will come for His bride. Jesus told His disciples, *"No one knows about that day or hour, not even the angels in heaven, nor the Son, but only the Father"* (Matthew 24:36). Once again, Jesus was using the "wedding talk" familiar to His listeners to convey the message of His second coming.

It's easy to overlook an important truth in this passage. It says only that no one knows the *day* or *hour*. It doesn't say that we can't know when the time is near.

Many well-meaning Bible teachers have taken this verse to mean we shouldn't try to discern when Jesus will come again. However, Jesus Himself said that we should learn to *"interpret the signs of the times"* (Matthew 16:3).

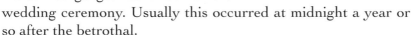

He also told us to look for these signs of his coming:

"There will be signs in the sun, moon and stars. On the earth, nations will be in anguish and perplexity at the roaring and tossing of the sea. Men will faint from terror, apprehensive of what is coming on the world, for the heavenly bodies will be shaken. At that time they will see the Son of Man coming in a cloud with power and great glory. When these things begin to take place, stand up and lift up your heads, because your redemption is drawing near."
—Luke 21:25–28

If God had not meant for us to discern when the time of the last days was near, He would not have given such specific prophecies in Scripture. The 70 weeks of Daniel (Daniel 9:2–27); the reference to the fig tree representing Israel (Luke 21:29–33); Jesus's discourse with His disciples concerning the end of the age (Matthew 24:1–51); and numerous other Scriptures teach us to watch for the signs that *"the kingdom of God is near"* (Luke 21:31).

Since the bride did not know when the wedding date would be or when her bridegroom would come for her, she watched for signs to see how the work on the bridal chamber was progressing. She also asked people close to the groom for hints concerning the status of the bridal chamber. The biblical bride remained in a constant state of readiness as she prepared herself for the wedding and waited for her groom.

In the same way, the bride of Christ must live expectantly for the day our Bridegroom comes to take us with Him: *"Therefore keep watch, because you do not know on what day your Lord will come"* (Matthew 24:42). Living in a constant state of readiness is part of the Christian pilgrimage through life.

Chosen and Cherished

Love-Letter Bouquet

"Be on guard! Be alert! You do not know when that time will come."
—Mark 13:33

What would you do to prepare for a wedding if you had no idea when it would take place?

What are you doing to prepare for your Bridegroom's Coming?

WAYS TO REMAIN WATCHFUL AND FAITHFUL

Remaining watchful for our Bridegroom is a lifelong task of the Christian. How can we keep watch and hold onto our faith?

God uses the physical realm we can understand to point to spiritual applications that often are more abstract. He created the earthly parallel of bride and bridegroom to teach us how to remain watchful and prepared for our heavenly Bridegroom. Preparing for our Bridegroom requires that we remain faithful to Him daily.

Scripture teaches us how we can remain faithful. Essentially, we must avoid idols and keep our focus on the truth, as God reveals in His Word. Please allow the Holy Spirit to speak to your heart concerning any ways you haven't been following God and commit to live more fully the abundant life Christ promised (John 10:10).

AVOIDING IDOLS

Any time we value anyone or anything more than we do God, we're involved in idolatry. *Merriam-Webster's 11th Collegiate Dictionary* defines idolatry as "the worship of a physical object as a god; an immoderate attachment or devotion to something."

Therefore, an idol is anyone or anything that hinders the love and trust we should have for God alone. It indicates a lack of faithfulness to our God.

Love-Letter Bouquet

Therefore, my dear friends, flee from idolatry.
— 1 Corinthians 10:14

Based on your present understanding of idolatry, is there anyone or anything that consumes your thought life more than Jesus?

If so, does that person or thing cause you to love God any less than you would if that person or thing were not part of your life?

The first reference to idols in the Bible is found in Genesis 31:19. When Jacob was fleeing from Laban, Rachel took her father's *household gods* and hid them in her camel's saddle. Thus, Jacob's beloved Rachel carried idols to the place they would settle.

Jacob's descendants fell into idol worship when they settled in Egypt. The 40 years of wandering in the wilderness brought them back to serving the one true God. God told them to destroy any traces of idolatry when they arrived in the Promised Land (Exodus 23:24). However, they adopted the pagan beliefs they encountered and worshipped idols in addition to worshipping the God of Israel (2 Chronicles 33:1–9). Their repeated disobedience led to the northern kingdom's exile to Assyria and the southern kingdom's exile to Babylon. During that time, many returned to following God.

Most cultures still practiced idol worship during New Testament days, as Paul encountered in Athens and other places (Acts 17:16–34). And many cultures still worship physical idols or other man-made images. However, as Christians we know idolatry can refers to a heart attitude and not just the actual worship of a physical object.

In Colossians 3:5, Paul refers to sexual immorality, impurity, lust, evil desires and greed as idolatry. Matthew 6:14 and Luke 16:31 equate the love of money with idolatry, stating you cannot serve money and God. Ephesians 5:5 (KJV) refers to covetousness as idolatry.

Love-Letter Bouquet

An increase in idolatry is a sign of the last days. Prayerfully read the following Scriptures:
- ❤ Romans 1:18–32
- ❤ 2 Timothy 3:1–7

Does either of these speak to you personally? If so, what will you do about it?

HOLDING TO THE TRUTH

Scripture warns that *"false Christs and false prophets will appear and perform signs and miracles to deceive the elect—if that were possible"* (Mark 13:22). As I travel and speak at different churches, I am finding an alarming trend. More and more people are espousing universalism and denying that the Cross is the only way of salvation. Jesus very plainly declared that He is the Way—not a way or our way—but *the* Way (John 14:6). Yet, even in some churches, Jesus's words are considered "narrow-minded," "exclusive," "judgmental," and "intolerant."

There are many concerns people express when confronted with the truth that Jesus is the world's only path to salvation. Often, those concerns take the form of questions regarding God's love for all humankind, His power, and His justice. There are a number of Scriptures helpful in addressing these questions: Jeremiah 29:13; 2 Chronicles 16:9a; Ecclesiastes 3:11; Luke 19:10; Romans 1:20; 2 Peter 3:9. I encourage you to read and study them, so that you can respond to people's questions with answers from God's Word.

I would like to briefly share a personal story that addresses these concerns as well. It illustrates God's love for all peoples and how He is always seeking the lost to become members of His church, His bride:

> One morning I received an unexpected call from a professor at a technical college asking me to teach remedial reading. I was astonished, as I had not even applied for such a position. When I went for the interview, I asked the professor how she got my name. She said, "I'm not sure. I was handed a list of names, and when I looked at the list, it were as though your name came off the page." Only later did I understand God's hand in it.
>
> One day after class, one of my students, a woman from Vietnam, asked to talk with me. I listened, enthralled, as she described her amazing escape from Vietnam years before. Then she went on to explain, "One day I went into my yard and a man was standing there bleeding. I said to him, 'Sir, you are hurt. I will help you.' I went inside to get rags and when I came out he was gone."
>
> She further explained that when she arrived in Thailand, she saw a crucifix and somehow knew that the man on the cross was the same man she had seen in her vision. She asked me, "Who was that man and why was he bleeding?"
>
> I had the blessed privilege of introducing her to Jesus. Later, she and her husband met with my husband, me, and a Vietnamese lay minister from the congregation our church sponsored. That day in my husband's office, two precious souls from a Buddhist background received Jesus as their only Savior!
>
> This experience confirmed to me how God longs for everyone to know Him, revealing Himself through dreams,

visions, and means we may never understand. Truly, those who seek Him will find Him.

Fundamentally, holding to the truth means holding to God's Word, the Bible. We can know that the God of the Bible, incarnate as Jesus Christ, is indeed the one true God and the only hope of our salvation. He confirms it in our hearts and He does so through His Word.

One powerful facet of that confirmation is the fulfillment of prophecy. The Bible tells us that God accurately predicts the future and reveals the history of the world from beginning to end. He has told us His plan for the world and those He created. God declares:

> *"I am the LORD; that is my name! I will not give my glory to another or my praise to idols. See, the former things have taken place, and new things I declare; before they spring into being I announce them to you."*
> —Isaiah 42:8–9

He even offers a challenge to those who believe in other gods:

> *"Bring in your idols to tell us what is going to happen. Tell us what the former things were, so that we may consider them and know their final outcome. Or declare to us the things to come, and tell us what the future holds, so we may know that you are gods."*
> —Isaiah 41:22–23

René Greenwood states that approximately 30 percent of the Bible is concerned with prophecy and the fulfillment of these prophecies is tied to God's reputation, His divinity and power ("Bible Prophecy Part 2," http://returnnow.org/2007/12/30/bible-prophecy-part-2-its-about-gods-reputation/). All the things that had a near fulfillment have happened just as He said (such as Jesus's incarnation, ministry, death, and resurrection; the destruction of Jerusalem; events described in Daniel 2). Those with a future fulfillment are still to come.

God's Word is true and will be accomplished. The Bible alone tells *"the end from the beginning,"* (Isaiah 46:10) and all that's in between. *"This is what the LORD says—Israel's King and Redeemer, the LORD Almighty: 'I am the first and I am the last; apart from me there is no God'"* (Isaiah 44:6). He is the one true and living God and He has chosen you to be His bride!

UNTIL THEN...

Until that glorious day when the Lord comes for His bride, let's keep our thoughts centered on our Bridegroom. *"'Let us rejoice and be glad and give him glory! For the wedding of the Lamb has come, and his bride has made herself ready'"* (Revelation 19:7). Let us watch and wait...until then!

PRAYER

Dear Lord, please help us always to remember who You are. While doing so, help us to remain faithful to You and Your Word...until then. In Jesus's name, amen.

INSIGHTS

THE COMING MESSIAH

Rosh Hashanah, the Feast of Trumpets, begins the Jewish New Year and is known as the wedding of the Messiah, according to WaitingforJesus.com. Rosh Hashanah occurs on a new moon, which comes about every 29.5 days on the lunar calendar. So, the new moon may occur either on the 29th or the 30th day after the last new moon. Since the time of the destruction of the Second Temple in Jerusalem in 70 A.D., Jewish tradition has been to celebrate Rosh Hashanah on two consecutive days, due to the difficulty of determining the new moon.

According to WaitingforJesus.com, "Of that day or hour no man knows" is an expression referring to this feast. Jesus's Jewish listeners in the first century would have understood His meaning when He correlated that wedding phrase with end-time events (His Second Coming) in Matthew 24.

Let's live expectantly, pondering the goodness of our Bridegroom. Let's do so each *day* and each *hour*!

(See http://www.waitingforjesus.com/jewishfeastprophecy.html)

PRAYER & PRAISE
JOURNAL

CHAPTER SEVEN

CLOTHED IN RIGHTEOUSNESS

By Edna Ellison

*I*n Bible times, an important part of the wedding process was securing and purifying the wedding garments. The chosen dress was washed in special soaps, dried and blocked carefully into shape, and hung in a special place, free of dust, until the time the groom came to claim his bride.

Grooms usually wore regal wedding crowns, and brides wore lovely veils and jeweled necklaces, anklets, bracelets, nose rings, and earrings. Similarly, today's bride spends time seeking just the right dress, shoes, and accessories for her wedding day.

About nine months before my daughter's June wedding, we began shopping for *the* dress. Patsy twirled in each dress as I circled her, my head under her armpit, looking for the price tag. One day Patsy said, "Mom, please stop leaning under my arm. It's embarrassing."

"I'm just checking the price, to see whether I like the dress...."

"How about this, Mom: if the dress costs over $500, I'll pay the difference, since I'm working now." We agreed. Then we prayed, asking God to give us a wedding dress with her favorite features—for $500.

One day in March, we found *the* dress. As Patsy stepped out of it, I dived into the pile of satin and lace for the price tag: $499.99! Thank you, Lord! Patsy paid a $50 deposit and the clerk ordered the dress, to be ready in several weeks. Meanwhile we celebrated His answer to our prayer.

In April, Patsy called me at work. "Mom," she sobbed. "You won't believe this. The bridal shop doesn't have my wedding dress. That style's been discontinued. They lost my phone number...couldn't let me know." She sniffed. "What are we going to do? It took six months to find this dress, and now we have only six weeks to find another one. It's hopeless!"

I responded with all the platitudes Christian mothers give: "Now, Patsy, we asked God for the perfect dress, for $500, didn't we?"

"Yes."

"Then we know He can provide another perfect dress, at that price, by June."

"Yes, Ma'am." She stopped crying.

As soon as we hung up, I felt empty. I realized I *myself* didn't even believe what I'd just said! Anger welled up inside. At the Christian ministry where I worked, I couldn't rail at God sitting at my desk, so I got *under* the desk and—I'm ashamed to say—shook my fist.

"Lord, how could You do this? I've bragged to everyone about your goodness and—You're not good today! Here I am, serving You, far from home, and my baby's crying! I can't hug her or comfort her. I've sacrificed for You, but You've broken my heart."

The next day at work the phone rang. Patsy said, "Mom, you won't believe this."

"What is it, Patsy?"

"I couldn't get my $50 back yesterday, so today when I came for it, I met the seamstress, who's going to alter the floor model— free! This shop will clean it and sell it to me for $250!"

I could hear her joy 400 miles away. After we hung up, I knew I owed God an apology, but I couldn't pray in my chair. I got back under the desk, on my knees. "O God, I'm sorry for the way I acted yesterday. You've always provided for my needs...and this time, You were busy saving me another $250! Lord, forgive me."

God had given us the best wedding dress as He clothed the bride—and her mother—in a *garment of trust*.

Love-Letter Bouquet

Physical wedding garments with decorations are merely a symbol of the rich spiritual garments we wear before Jesus, our Bridegroom. The Bible often suggests clothing as a symbol of spiritual truths.

Read Matthew 22:11–13. What did the king who had given the wedding dinner for his son notice about the unknown guest?

In an average Jewish community, like the ones Jesus described in His parables, everyone enjoyed and celebrated weddings. In this story, after the proposal, the long waiting period of anticipation, and the loud processional through the streets to bring the bride to the groom's house, everyone knew about the wedding. If this is true, why do you think the man was invited but then not accepted as a wedding guest?

Describe the outside area, where the guest was thrown (Matthew 22:13).

Compare Matthew 22:11–13 with Matthew 13:40–42 and 25:30. What might these areas outside symbolize?

Revelation 19:7–8 tells us about a beautiful, clean wedding dress, a symbol of the righteous acts of Christians. *"For the wedding of the Lamb has come, and his bride has made herself ready. Fine linen, bright and clean, was given her to wear.' (Fine linen stands for the righteous acts of the saints.)"* In your daily life, what kinds of acts would you consider righteous? Who has given us the fine linen (even the righteous acts) we are to wear?

PURE AND SPOTLESS

According to Anita Diamant in *The New Jewish Wedding*, "In Jewish practice the wearing of white has as much to do with spiritual purity as physical virginity. A wedding is considered a personal Yom Kippur, a day of repentance and forgiveness for the couple. Among Orthodox Jews the bride's white dress indicates that she has been to the mikvah, the ritual bath, in preparation for the wedding, and the groom's kittle (a short white linen robe bound by a white belt and worn over his suit) represents his spiritual readiness for marriage."

Having already observed the mikvah, the bride would be wearing a spotless dress, without defect or stain. *"All beautiful you are, my darling; there is no flaw in you"* (Song of Songs 4:7). Throughout the Bible, we read passages about offerings to God without defect or blemish. One requirement for Jesus, the Lamb of God, was that He had no flaw, no sin, fulfilling the Old Testament requirement for a perfect lamb as a sacrifice. *"Blessed are those who wash their robes, that they may…go through the gates into the city"* (Revelation 22:14). The bride would have been vigilant to keep her wedding garment clean, unwrinkled, and ready for the wedding at a moment's notice. Now she wore it at the formal ceremony, like a queen, the center of attention.

Love-Letter Bouquet

Read the following Scriptures and explain how you think they apply to you as part of the church, acceptable as the bride of Christ.

- ❤ Leviticus 21:10, 13, 16, 23
- ❤ Numbers 19:2
- ❤ Daniel 1:4
- ❤ Ephesians 5:27
- ❤ 1 Peter 1:19
- ❤ Proverbs 31:22–25

Read Ephesians 1:4–8. What really qualifies Christians to be holy and blameless before God in heaven? Pray now, thanking God for providing Jesus as your Savior.

ALL DECKED OUT IN JEWELS

As discussed earlier, the groom gave the bride a simple ring at the betrothal. It was a clear indication that she was his, legally and spiritually. At the wedding ceremony, she wore that plain ring, worth only an inexpensive coin. Its small value insured the couple did not get their priorities out of order, but that the ring was more important spiritually—as a sign of their covenant with each other and with God—than it was as valuable jewelry. Today many brides wear a plain gold or precious metal band closer to the heart than the engagement ring, which is more expensive but used as a protection on the outside of the bride's finger, shielding the plain wedding band, the most important ring.

The bride's other jewelry was usually ornate, filled with as many jewels as both families could afford. Though she may have been shy, her outfit was breathtaking! John describes his vision: *"I saw the Holy City, the new Jerusalem, coming down out of heaven from God, prepared as a bride beautifully dressed for her husband"* (Revelation 21:2).

Wendy Ellison, my daughter-in-law, asked one of her best friends to sing "How Beautiful" by Twila Paris as a wedding solo during her marriage to my son, Jack. One of the most beautiful lines speaks of the church as Christ's radiant bride "who waits for her Groom with His light in her eyes." Wendy was beautiful during the evening wedding as her eyes reflected her love for Jack and his love for her.

Love-Letter Bouquet

Read Matthew 9:16. The Bible compares an old, worn-out garment to a new one. In this story, the old garment that needs patching represents whom? The fresh garment represents whom? Why won't the new patch be appropriate for the old garment?

Reflections

Have you ever sewn anything with cloth that has not been preshrunk? What happened?

Sometimes, as the bride of Christ, without knowing all we should about our Lord, we grab swatches of theology and doctrine from here and there and patch them into something we already know. Our mistakes and errors in thinking can be a misfit as we dress in holiness for our Groom. Have you ever felt like a Christian misfit? Colossians 2:2–3 has an answer to the situation. Who has all wisdom and all knowledge? How can you obtain new life and new knowledge?

Do Clothes Make the Man? Or Woman?

In American Westerns, the hero, usually the town sheriff, dresses in a white hat and faces down Black Bart, a mean hombre in a black hat. While clothing has no miraculous powers, we use attire to stereotype the character of heroes who live by the "code of the West" and others who don't. In a similar manner, clothing often takes on symbolic meaning throughout the Bible.

O Lord . . . you are clothed with splendor and majesty.
—Psalm 104:1

"May your priests be clothed with righteousness."—Psalm 132:9

Clothe yourselves with humility toward one another.—1 Peter 5:5

We groan, longing to be clothed with our heavenly dwelling.
—2 Corinthians 5:2–4

I delight greatly in the Lord. . . . For he has clothed me with garments of salvation and arrayed me in a robe of righteousness, as a bridegroom adorns his head like a priest, and as a bride adorns herself with her jewels. — Isaiah 61:10

"You have a few people in Sardis, who have not soiled their clothes. They will walk with me, dressed in white, for they are worthy. He who overcomes will, like them, be dressed in white." — Revelation 3:4–5 (See also Revelation 4:4; 7:9; and 15:6.)

Garments may also symbolize evil character.

"Wolves dressed in sheep's clothing." — Matthew 7:15
He wore cursing as his garment. — Psalm 109:18
My accusers will be clothed with disgrace and wrapped in shame as in a cloak. — Psalm 109:29
Jeremiah condemns prostitutes *"dressed in scarlet with jewels of gold."* — Jeremiah 4:30

Then there's the miraculous story of a sick woman who was healed in Matthew 5:25–34. Jesus did not touch her, and neither did she touch Him. She only touched the edge of His garment. We know from the crucifixion story (John 19:23–24) that Jesus's robe was unusual, without seams, woven in one piece from top to bottom. The Roman soldiers at the foot of the Cross gambled for it because they didn't want to tear the magnificent garment into several pieces. As they cast lots for it, they fulfilled the prophecy in Psalm 22:18: *"They divide my garments among them and cast lots for my clothing."*

In spite of this unusual robe, it had no miraculous power as the woman touched the hem. The power came from Jesus, who was spiritually *"clothed in splendor and majesty"* (Psalm 104:1) as He demonstrated His power to heal us from every sickness, sin, and death—permanently. His miraculous touch was not needed on earth, because it was bigger than earth; it was fulfilled in the greatest sense in His resurrection, and that personal, spiritual touch for each of us still remains at the right hand of God in heaven, always available for you and me.

Love-Letter Bouquet

Read Isaiah 61:10. How do you know Jesus has provided for you the *"garment of salvation"*? How do you see evidence (in others and in yourself) that He purifies Christians to be worthy of heaven?

In your experience, has it been instant purification, progressive, or both?

Praise God that He loves us just as we are, and we can enter heaven by faith, believing on Him and His righteousness as the Son of God.

PRAYER

O Lord and Savior, because of Your sacrifice, we stand before You in spiritual white linen, pure and blameless, washed in the blood of the Lamb. Thank You for Your great sacrifice for us, Your church, Your bride. Dress us in strength and dignity as we stand in the ashes of humility and offer You the sacrifice of a daily life of service. Purify us, O God, and make us fit for heaven. Amen.

INSIGHTS

DIVERSE TRADITIONS

Different cultures have different traditions regarding the wedding dress. From my friends in English as a Second Language classes at my church I got a traditional Asian perspective on attire for the big day:

Chinese and Cambodian brides often wear bright red dresses for their weddings. Some of my Chinese and Cambodian bride friends tell me their cultures feel the color red brings good luck. At times they tell me a bride will wear two dresses on her wedding day: a white dress for a secular ceremony after the religious one with the red dress. Chinese and Japanese women may spend extravagant amounts of money on wedding garments, often with designers commissioned to make a spectacular dress of embroidered satin in red, white, or another color. Korean wedding dresses can come in many colors as well, with a raised empire waist and dainty pointed sleeves. Japanese brides who wish to follow ancient traditions wear embroidered, kimono-style gowns with straight, boxy lines. The groom wears a similar gown, except that his has a beautifully shaped waistline!

No matter what the bride (or groom) wears, the beauty of the clothing and the care taken in its selection and preparation are merely a reflection of the importance of the wedding ceremony. And our ceremonies now are only the slightest taste of the wonderful, future, and eternal wedding feast of the Lamb and His bride.

Chosen and Cherished

PRAYER & PRAISE
JOURNAL

CHAPTER EIGHT

THE BIG DAY ARRIVES

By Kimberly Sowell with Edna Ellison

I t was the big day for the blushing bride. She and her groom had planned to marry the day before, but their blood work was a day late. When Howard arrived, Mary smoothed out the creases in her mink-collared beige woolen suit, kissed her mother on the cheek, grabbed her bags, and headed out the door. She had already bid her daddy farewell that morning as he headed off for work. Mary and Howard set their sights on the little church where they were to be married by their beloved pastor, with his wife as a witness.

Were their parents boycotting the wedding? No, they simply had to work that day. And the bride's and groom's friends? They wished them well from afar, because they hadn't been invited. Mary and Howard drove to the church, said "I do" to one another, and continue today to live happily ever after.

For years I was horrified that my parents (Mary and Howard Sowell) had taken such a simplistic approach to their wedding ceremony. I did not understand why their parents would not stave off their chores for even one day to see their children get married. And how could my mother bear being deprived the honor of walking down the aisle while family and friends admired her beautifully adorned satin gown? No flower girl, no tossing of the bouquet — my parents had been robbed of their moment in the spotlight, and yet this was how they planned it! And their explanation? In their home community, a wedding with invited guests during that time period would have been considered "showing off." My parents recall their wedding day with great fondness, and their 46-year marriage has yet to suffer from the absence of bridesmaids and a towering cake on their wedding day.

I didn't choose to follow my parents' model for the perfect wedding. Instead, for ten months I selected flowers for the bouquets, considered finger foods for the reception tables, searched for the perfect cake topper, attended countless dress alteration sessions, poured over a mountain of bridesmaid dress catalogs to select a dress suiting all the bridal party's shapes, listened to stacks of organ music, and fretted over every detail of the whole affair. At first, the planning was fairy tale fun, but the process soon became drudgery and a great source of stress. On many days, it was hard to keep in mind the true meaning behind all the planning—the initiation of a marriage relationship with my dear husband-to-be.

In American culture, families plan weddings for months in advance. The bride is the center of attention, the majority of the money for the wedding is spent on pleasing guests, the groom goes along with the wishes of the bride if he knows what's good for him, and the meaning behind the grand event is... well, understood. But strip away the guest list, the fancy reception, the elaborate clothes, and the floral displays, and what's left is all that matters—a man and a woman pledging their lives to one another. The vows are all that matter, because without the pledge of the bride and groom, the wedding is nothing more than an overpriced party.

REVELRY IN THE STREETS

In Bible times, the bride waited for her groom to prepare a place in his father's house for her (usually around a year). Once the groom completed the newlywed wing of his father's house, the father inspected it. Then he gave the groom the signal to go claim his bride, romantically steal her away, and take her to her new home. The bride had been waiting in anticipation, with her wedding garments constantly cleaned and ready for the processional. The sound of a shofar blown by the groom's entourage awakened the whole community. They came out into the streets, where the groom, his best man, and other family members gained entrance into the bride's home and escorted her down the streets to her new home. She was accompanied by maidens (today's bridesmaids) or family, who danced, sang, and rejoiced as they traveled.

Sometimes four honored guests carried the *huppah* (sometimes spelled *chuppah*), the tent without side walls, held up by four poles.

The bride and groom, treated as a king and queen, walked under the huppah to the groom's house and others reveled and celebrated alongside them. As soon as the bride arrived at the groom's house, the wedding ceremony began. Afterward, the couple observed a week of intimacy in which the marriage was consummated (see chapter 9), and then the wedding feast began.

Love-Letter Bouquet

Paul explains to the church at Corinth how Christ will return to claim His bride, the church, and take her to His Father's house in heaven. Read 1 Corinthians 15:50–57, looking at the following elements of the wedding processional and how they relate to these verses:

💜 The state of Christians when the call comes (v. 51)
💜 Sound to call the bride to her new home (v. 52)
💜 Change to clean clothes (v. 53)
💜 Rebirth of hope and new beginnings (v. 54–55)

Read Revelation 19:6–9,11–14, 17 and compare the wedding symbols with those above in 1 Corinthians 15. List wedding imagery in Revelation 19:13–17 and Matthew 24:30–31.

Read John 14:1–4. How does Jesus, like the Bridegroom in other passages, give you comfort?

Reflections

In your own words, describe what Jesus's promises in John 14 mean to you.

BEING READY

In His parable of the ten virgins (Matthew 25:1–13), Jesus gave a good illustration of the readiness that should characterize His bride, the church. Five of the ten virgins (who could be called "tired or distracted bridesmaids" today) were foolish, and five of them were wise. As you read this passage, think of your situation in today's busy world. How are you like the wise bridesmaids? Like the foolish ones? Have you, like them, ever been late to an important event? Have you made a habit of being late, careless, or distracted from spiritual matters? Are you guarding your times alone with God? Do you think Jesus notices? May we Christians keep vigilant as we await our Groom coming from heaven!

Love-Letter Bouquet

Read Matthew 25:1–13. Why did the bridesmaids fall asleep? (Matthew 25:5) When did they awaken? (v. 6) Did a trumpet sound wake them?

Why did the wise bridesmaids refuse to give the foolish ones their oil? (v. 9)

What happened at the end of the story? (vv. 10–12)

Reflections

Just as the wise bridesmaids took an extra container of oil since they didn't know when the groom would come, you and I should give extra time and attention to preparing for Christ's coming. When the groom suddenly appeared at midnight, the foolish bridesmaids asked the other girls to give them oil, but there was not enough to share.
How would you have felt if you were one of the foolish ones?

How would you have felt if you were one of the wise ones?

What words of advice could you give to non-Christians who, at this time, would not be ready for the Bridegroom's coming?

CUSTOMS OF THE TENT

In Old Testament times the nomadic tribes of Israel performed the wedding ceremony in the tents of the groom's family. In later years, when Jewish families lived in houses (usually with dirt floors), they kept the tradition of the tent of covering over the bride and groom. The huppah (see definition above) was central to the marriage ceremony. Sometimes rabbis who led the ceremony didn't even come under the tent; it was a holy place for the bride and groom. In some places no official religious leader participated in the ceremony. The central focus was on the decisions of the bride and groom.

The Everything Jewish Wedding Book by Rabbi Hyim Shafner tells us the open huppah is reminiscent of Abraham's tent, which was just a covering without sides to show that anyone, from any direction, was welcomed into his home. In modern Jewish weddings, sometimes the groom takes his prayer shawl and wraps it around his bride, to symbolize the huppah.

Love-Letter Bouquet

Read the following Scriptures and discuss with a friend how these ancient stories are related to the idea of *huppah*. Match the Scripture reference with the ideas at the right.

Ruth 3:1–9   God's banner over you is pure love.

Song of Songs 2:4   God covered even the unfaithful and forgotten.

Isaiah 61:10   Covering a woman obligated a man to marriage.

Ezekiel 16:8–12   God clothes you with salvation and righteousness.

Chosen and Cherished

Blessed Are You, God

When the wedding ceremony itself began, the ritual blessing of the cups was repeated as a remembrance of the betrothal ceremony. According to Rabbi Shafner's *The Everything Jewish Wedding Book*, in some traditions, the bride circles around her groom several times (at least three and up to seven times) as He takes her under the huppah. Her actions symbolize the forming of "walls" of protection for the family and new home.

This is followed today by seven blessings, which are pronounced in the presence of witnesses. According to ancient tradition, the seven blessings celebrate God and His creation: the fruit of the vine (wine); the universe (everything for His glory); humanity; the forming of humanity in His image; the people of Israel and their return to Zion; loving companionship and human joy, specifically that of bride and groom; and the gladness of the time of messianic redemption. Each blessing begins with these words: "Blessed are You, God, Sovereign of the universe."

After the blessings, post-biblical Jewish tradition dictates that a glass be broken (wrapped in something to avoid injury), which commemorates the destruction of Jerusalem. Rabbi Shafner writes, "Breaking something at the moment of our greatest joy is a profound statement that though for us personally we may feel all is whole and joyous, for the larger world in general and for our people in particular, all is not wholeness and peace."

The breaking of the glass indicates the beginning of the marriage-supper festivities. Twenty-first century wedding guests celebrate the sound of breaking glass with a shout of "Mazel tov!" (Good luck!)

Too Busy to Keep Intimacy with Jesus

Spend a moment taking stock of what really matters in your Christian walk. Peel away all the layers of your ministry activities, church services, committee meetings, and special projects. Remove yourself for a moment from your relationship with the church. Now move beyond the outward actions in response to Christ in your life; how you express Christ in your life; even beyond the means by which you strive to become more like Christ. Let's get down to bare walls, a simplistic approach, to consider only you and the Lord Jesus and who you are to each other. This is where personal relationship and faith begins. As you gaze into the eyes of the Savior, do you see yourself in the reflection of His eyes? Have you become one with the Lord? Have you hidden yourself in Him, died to self, surrendered your all to Him, and received Him as He has extended His hand of mercy, grace, and love?

We can become easily misdirected in our Christian walk, as any bride can be distracted by all the secondary accoutrements of her wedding. We know the entire wedding event is centered around the exchange of the vows, yet as layer upon layer of wedding planning takes place, our focus can shift to the extras so much so that they overshadow the day's true significance. As we seek to serve the Lord through ministry involvement, Bible studies, and other church-related activities, we can become so focused on all the doing and going that we let our focus slip away from the foundation of why we do these things: a relationship with Jesus. Just as a wedding can become drudgery for the bride who gets lost in a sea of fabric swatches and invitations, the Christian walk can become a laborious chore for those who allow Christianity to become just one big to-do list. Just as a wedding with no exchange of vows is void and pointless, church work and ministry is meaningless without a personal relationship with Jesus Christ.

If you've accepted Jesus as your personal Savior, truly you are the bride of Christ. Do you ever find yourself feeling like an overstressed bride? Have your joy and enthusiasm turned to stress and frustration? Your labor of love into a dreaded obligation? Consider Mary and Howard's wedding approach and apply their approach to your life. Remind yourself: your first love must be the Lord Jesus, and all ministry must flow out of a deep love relationship with Him. Ask God to help you discern His will for your life. Be willing to stay when He says stay. Trust Him enough to move when He sends you forward, even if there's more work to be accomplished. Do nothing out of a desire to show others how committed you are or how gifted God has made you, but be motivated only by your love for Jesus, which propels you into action when you hear that still small voice.

Chosen and Cherished

PRAYER

Lord, help us not be misdirected in our Christian walk, but to focus on You, our Bridegroom, and accept Your covering over us with love. As we join You in a personal covenant relationship, help us be ever ready to listen for Your call. Amen.

INSIGHTS

IT'S IN THE DETAILS

My friends, the Coopers, rushed to finish all the last-minute details in preparation for their daughter's wedding ceremony. They dressed her in a fashionable wedding dress. They arrived at the church a few minutes early, double checking with the church's wedding director about the cake, the reception hall, the band, and the candles. As they began checking off each item, they questioned the ring bearer, who had no rings. All the wedding party looked at the bride's mother and agreed it was her responsibility, yet the rings were still at home.

"It's my responsibility?" she said with disbelief.

"Yes," responded the other family members, looking away with an innocent stare.

With no time to spare, she drove home, about five minutes away, retrieved the rings, and returned just in time to give them to the ring bearer and to be escorted down the aisle to the bride's mother's seat on the first pew.

In today's world we have become casual about many events, but religious wedding ceremonies are not one of those. Families in most Christian weddings will do almost anything to make sure all the details are in order for the sacred event!

May all Christian brides and their families be even more careful about the details of their spiritual lives, daily guarding their sacred intimacy to our precious Bridegroom, Christ the Lord.

—Edna Ellison

PRAYER & PRAISE
JOURNAL

CHAPTER NINE

THE JOY OF INTIMACY

By Joy Brown

hen I speak at conferences, I often use anecdotes from my years of teaching deaf children. For instance, in order to help develop the concept of "words" in preschoolers, I would move from physical objects to the more abstract written word for the object. I usually began with the word *ball*. I had various types of balls—Nerf ball, beach ball, dodge ball—available to play with the children. We rolled them, gently threw them, and played games with them. Then we looked at pictures of balls. I progressed to showing the sign language and finger spelling for

the word, and then finally to the printed word "ball" in books. All the while, I was moving from concrete to abstract.

The same is true of the way God often teaches us in the Bible. Our all-wise, loving God knows how we learn. So He uses physical lessons, which are more easily understood, to teach us spiritual truths that may be more difficult for us to comprehend. Grasping the beauty of this chapter's key concept—the consummation of the marriage—may require some creative thinking, but it will be well worth the effort.

THE SIGNIFICANCE OF THE BRIDAL CHAMBER

The bridal chamber is certainly a foreign concept for today's society, but it was a special part of the biblical wedding. After the wedding ceremony was complete and the couple had gone to the father's house, they entered the newly prepared bridal chamber alone to consummate the marriage. The groom's friend (or "best man" in today's society) stood outside the door and waited. When the couple had consummated the marriage, the bridegroom announced it to his waiting friend: *"The bride belongs to the bridegroom. The friend who attends the bridegroom waits and listens for him, and is full of joy when he hears the bridegroom's voice"* (John 3:29). The groom's friend in turn announced to the waiting crowd outside that the couple now was united. Afterwards, the waiting guests began to celebrate the covenant marriage.

The bridegroom and his new bride usually remained in the bridal chamber for a week. When they emerged from the chamber, the marriage supper feast began. John's gospel records Jesus's first miracle (turning the water into wine) as taking place at a marriage supper (John 2:1–11).

APPLICATION FOR THE BRIDE OF CHRIST TODAY

You may be wondering, "How in the world does this custom relate to me as the bride of Christ today?" Keep in mind once again that God uses the physical to point us to spiritual truths.

Interestingly, the Hebrew word used to convey the physical act of sex is *yada,* which means "to know" in the sense of "to experience." Certainly, to *"be fruitful and increase in number"* (Genesis 1:28) is one purpose of the sexual act. However, the real goal of the physical act is intimacy. This physical experience, which allows a married couple the most intimate understanding of each other possible, hints at the depth of intimacy and understanding we can spiritually experience with our Bridegroom.

Love-Letter Bouquet

"Blessed is the man you discipline, O LORD, the man you teach from your law."
—Psalm 94:12

In the following Scriptures, how does God teach us spiritual truths through physical objects or occurrences?
- ♥ John 3:3
- ♥ John 4:10
- ♥ Ephesians 6:11

Our Future Hope

One day we will be in the full presence of our Bridegroom: "'*Let us rejoice and be glad and give him glory! For the wedding of the Lamb has come, and his bride has made herself ready*'" (Revelation 19:7). Then and only then will we discover how wonderful He truly is!

We will have eternity to learn how deeply He loves us and discover all the many ways He has shown that love. We will learn how He allowed all things to "*work together for good*" (Romans 8:28) in our lives.

As a youth, I was taught that when we get to heaven we'll have full knowledge. However, as I observe the joy my grandbabies Ty and Mazi Grace experience as they learn new things, I now believe our experience will be one of progressive revelation—learning and growing for eternity. Just think how wonderful it will be to learn how events in our lives fit together, how many times we were protected when we didn't know it, and how various people were placed in our lives at just the right moment! Just think how wonderful it will be to learn how He prepared our eternal homes and the care He took in choosing a special name known only unto Him! (Revelation 2:17). Just think how humbling it will be to learn how great a price He really paid for us to be His bride!

Developing Intimacy with Jesus

Until that day, when we are fully in His presence, we can grow in our understanding of Him and develop deeper spiritual intimacy here on earth. Just as in most societies couples "court" or "date" before they marry to get to know each other, we can court our Bridegroom. The following are some suggestions of how to do that. Enjoy this section as you fall in love with the King of Hearts.

"Let me introduce myself": In Western society the initial stage of courtship begins, at some point, with an introduction. Even if you begin dating someone you've known for years, earlier you either had introduced yourselves to each other or someone introduced you.

My husband, Wayne, and I met at a sock hop when we were teenagers. Our county had only two high schools, but they were ten miles apart. A sock hop was held monthly at the National Guard Armory to bring the teenagers from both schools together for an event. One night, the disc jockey, Bill Gibbons, called for a "Paul Jones" dance. The girls came forward and formed a circle facing outward. The boys surrounded them and formed a circle facing inward. When the music started, the girls moved clockwise and the boys moved counterclockwise.

As the circles were moving around each other, Bill often stopped the music and said, "Paul Jones." You then danced with the person in front of you. About the third "Paul Jones," Wayne and I faced each other. Since we knew we only had a short amount of time, we quickly introduced ourselves before "Paul Jones" was called out again. Today we both love to reflect on that first time we saw each other and the short but sweet introduction.

Love-Letter Bouquet

Read Psalm 139:1–24. The Bridegroom already knows everything about you, but He enjoys hearing your deepest thoughts. In the space below, write an introduction of yourself to Jesus. Be honest with how you feel about yourself.

We hear often, "You never get a second chance to make a first impression." However, that adage is not true with our Bridegroom. Even if you feel you have completely failed — with wrong choices in life — He loves you anyway and lets you start over each day: *"Because of the LORD's great love we are not consumed, for his compassions never fail. They are new every morning; great is your faithfulness"* (Lamentations 3:22–23). Do you grasp the good news in this verse? It's as though each morning He gives you another chance to introduce yourself to Him! What will be your introduction today? What would you like for it to be tomorrow? Write down you thoughts below.

Reflections

Try this, just for fun: Imagine you have just arrived in heaven. Your eyes behold myriads of angels and beauty too wonderful to express. Look around you and see loved ones who have been waiting for you. Your pulse quickens as you see them, one by one! Linger there a moment and imagine what you will say or feel. Then, you turn and catch the first glimpse of your Bridegroom face-to-face. What do you think your first words to Him will be?

Spend a few moments dreaming about heaven! Write a praise-phrase, a spiritual love poem, a song, or a journal entry about what you think you'll find in heaven. Save it as a precious memento of your study of this book.

"I'd like to get to know you": Generally, the second stage of courtship is getting to know each other's likes and dislikes, their hopes and desires. This stage is an exciting part of the overall process. You can discover much about a person's character and personality by learning about his or her passions, desires, and dreams. As we learn more about our Groom-to-be and begin to understand His heart, our desires should begin to align with His.

Love-Letter Bouquet

Read Proverbs 6:17 to learn seven things our Bridegroom
dislikes. In fact, He hates them. List them below.

1.

2.

3.

4.

5.

6.

7.

Now, beside each word, make a list of seven things that
you dislike. How does your list compare to His? Are you
compatible?

"I'm falling in love with you": In many cases, a couple's love will
develop and deepen with time, leading to marriage. "Falling in love"
is simply wanting what's best for the other person rather than for
yourself. Yes, wonderful, happy emotions accompany it, but the
most important part of the relationship is sacrificial love. Have you
fallen in love with and accepted the love of the Bridegroom? That's
the most important question you'll answer in life.

Several years ago, a young man went forward during the
invitation at a storefront church. He'd been a Christian for many
years; however, as the pastor had preached about experiencing
God's love, he knelt and humbly prayed for God to show him His
love.

Chosen and Cherished

What happened at that altar was so dramatic that he stood back to his feet a different man. He had known *intellectually* that God loved him, and he had responded to that love when he accepted Christ. However, when he *spiritually* accepted God's love that act changed his life.

Some time later he was relating this story to his former Sunday school teacher. He looked at her and asked, "Have you ever experienced God's love?"

"Oh, yes," was her natural response.

Over the following weeks, the Sunday school teacher kept thinking about his question. "Have you ever experienced God's love?" She finally had the courage to ask, "Lord, have I?"

God immediately began to show her misconceptions about Him she had harbored. She had been so devoted to Him—trying to please Him and to meet what she thought were His expectations—that she spent little time with Him. The hardest thing she had to admit was that she was afraid of God. She'd lived with a sense of dread that He was waiting to send judgment on her at any moment. She feared that if she prayed, "Thy will be done," some horrible calamity would strike her, her family, or both.

This Sunday school teacher was astonished by her misconceptions about God. She, like the young man, prayed, "Lord, let me experience Your love." I know this story is true. I was the Sunday school teacher.

We live in such a task-oriented world that we're prone to believe we have to merit God's love. When I realized that nothing I ever could do would cause God to love me *any less or any more*, this recognition transformed my life, too.

Love-Letter Bouquet

Read Romans 8:1–4, 28–39. Allow the Holy Spirit to use these words to speak to your heart. Record the responses that immediately come to mind as a result. Draw hearts beside the responses that mean the most to you at this time in your life.

Reflections

What do you feel is threatening to separate you from the love of God in Christ Jesus? According to Romans 8:38–39, does it have that power?

PRAYER

Dear Lord, may the words we've written above be the prayer of our hearts. Help us remain in love with You and grow deeper still with passionate love for You as our Savior-Bridegroom. In Jesus's name, amen.

Insights

Once a couple has fallen in love, they need to find ways to keep that love fresh and alive. Part of that journey is looking out for two issues that cause most problems in relationships: miscommunication and misperception.

God has clearly communicated His love to us. However, our perceptions of that love can easily become distorted or clouded over time.

I was raised in a Christian home and had accepted Christ at a young age. I was passionate about Him. Even as a third grader, I would make sentences from my spelling words telling about Him. I attended church every time I possibly could. During the altar call at church, if I sensed someone was under the conviction of the Holy Spirit, I would walk up to them and ask, "Would you like me to walk down the aisle with you?" I laugh when I think about how irritating I must have been to the adults in my church.

With time, I noticed that my passion did not seem "normal" in most situations, so I began to cool down to try to be more like others. After a time of deep soul-searching in my late 20s, I experienced a renewal of my passion through the work of the Holy Spirit.

Everything seemed brand new. I had fallen head over heels in love with the Bridegroom once again. God's Word came alive. Prayer times were powerful. I often sat in church crying during the singing of the same hymns I'd sung for years. The words had new meaning.

The evangelist Vance Havner once said, "The church is so subnormal that if it ever got back to the New Testament normal it would seem to people to be abnormal." I have taken this message as a life challenge. And it must resonate with others as well, because when I was recently interviewed about my spiritual journey the local magazine editor entitled the published article, "Never Subnormal Again."

Enjoy the journey of life as you wait for the day when you will be in the full presence of the Bridegroom forever. Until that day, will you determine never to be "subnormal" in your passion for Him while here on earth?

PRAYER & PRAISE
JOURNAL

CHAPTER TEN

LET THE CELEBRATION BEGIN!

By Kimberly Sowell

T he Bible describes numerous occasions on which God's people celebrated His goodness. Leviticus is filled with instructions on celebrations and feasts, such as the Feast of Trumpets, the Feast of Atonement, the Feast of Firstfruits, the Feast of Tabernacles, the Feast of Unleavened Bread (including Passover), and the Year of Jubilee Feasts. Feasts were observed near Mount Sinai (Exodus 23:14–17), in the wilderness (Numbers 9:3–5), and at the beginning of the conquest of the Promised Land (Joshua 5:10, 11). It seems at any excuse, the Israelites killed a fatted calf and had a festival of rejoicing!

A well-known illustration is the story of the Prodigal Son in Luke 15. As soon as the wandering son returned, the father asked for his best outfit for his son to wear. Then he told the servants: *"'Bring the fattened calf and kill it. Let's have a feast and celebrate'…so they began to celebrate"* (vv. 23–24). It was only after the older son, working hard in the fields, heard the loud music and dancing (v. 25), that he came to see what was happening and became jealous of his brother!

A wedding in those days was a popular cause for celebration. After the ceremony and physical consummation of the marriage, while the bride and groom were in the bridal chamber sharing a week or more of private time—similar to a contemporary honeymoon—their extended families enjoyed a celebration feast. When the couple came out of the bridal chamber, an even greater feast began! Everyone partook of plentiful wine and food, and families reveled in exuberant music, laughter, and dancing. They also shared oral traditions and family histories, getting to know each other better.

Love-Letter Bouquet

Read Philippians 4:4–8. Can you say you are joyful when you think of your spiritual life?

How long has it been since you rejoiced and celebrated your church fellowship?

Reflections

In your busy life with car pools, church organizations, and secular meetings, how can you make time for joyful moments of celebration with your Lord at church or at home?

How long has it been since you rejoiced over your personal fellowship with the Lord?

Are you feeding on the feast of His Word?

Ask God to show you how to grow more joyful and celebrate that spirit with family and church members.

Getting to Know Each Other

One of the most joyous traditions in any Jewish family was (is) their celebration of marriage! A master of ceremonies at the marriage supper, or wedding feast, kept the merriment going among guests. Their laughter and deep joy ideally reflected the joy of the couple, who were growing closer each day, as they intimately shared their lives and family traditions with each other. In some cases, leaders of various tribes and families made peace as their daughters and sons married, promising common grandchildren between the two factions and creating a period of peace and friendship among them. (See 2 Chronicles 8:11 and 11:23.) Getting to know each other face-to-face helped them to understand each other's customs and characteristics in a more personal way.

Have you noticed that when you get to know others it is hard to harbor past prejudices or stereotypes? As we come together as families, we celebrate the melding of common traditions, stories, and ancestry. As we join as fellow Christians in the family of God, again our prejudices should dissolve away as we get to know each other.

When I first met Tricia Scribner, I wasn't sure I'd like her. After several months of being the only woman in my seminary classes in Charlotte, I was accustomed to representing all womankind among my peers. Then suddenly Tricia arrived on the scene. The professor announced she was a writer. *Humph.* I wanted to be a writer. He also said she was a speaker. *Humph.* I was a speaker. And she asked such intelligent questions, revealing great depth of understanding. *Humph.* She was a sharp cookie. I wanted to be the sharp cookie. I supposed such a smart lady must be intense all the time.

Was I wrong! Not about her intelligence, but I had no idea she was also such a warm, caring, fun-loving gal. I thought I knew her from watching her from afar, but it wasn't until I spent time with her that I could even begin to understand her. After several years now, I still continue to learn more about the wonderful ways of my friend Tricia Scribner.

To become intimately acquainted with someone, you must spend time with that person. After talking about various topics over several hours, you begin to understand how she thinks. Then as you go through various experiences together, you begin to know how she typically acts. You begin to know her beliefs, her character, and other nuances that compose who she is. And if you find her ways to be beautiful and pleasing, you will grow to love this friend.

Do you know anyone that intimately? Does anyone know you that well? Of course, because God knows all, sees all, and can decipher the intents of a person's heart, we realize He knows us more intimately than we know ourselves; we sometimes can deceive ourselves, but we can't deceive God. But how well do you *know* God? Jesus is your Bridegroom if you are a Christian, and you are His Bride. As you wait for His return, are you becoming more intimately acquainted with Him?

Getting to Know God

God established the marital relationship of the harlot Gomer and the prophet Hosea as a representation of the rocky relationship between Israel and her God. In the book of Hosea, God brought many charges against Israel, His chosen people. We know that as Christians, we are also His people, His chosen bride. God wants His chosen ones to know Him. He has said, *"I will betroth you to Me in faithfulness, and you shall know the Lord"* (Hosea 2:20 NKJV). Yet, throughout the book of Hosea we find a constant accusation against Israel that they did not know their God: *"Hear the word of the Lord, you children of Israel, for the Lord brings a charge against the inhabitants of the land: 'There is no truth or mercy or knowledge of God in the land'"* (Hosea 4:1 NKJV). And again: *"'They do not direct their deeds toward turning to their God, for the spirit of harlotry is in their midst, and they do not know the Lord'"* (Hosea 5:4 NKJV).

He rescued them, protected them, fed and cared for them, yet they knew Him not. This greatly displeased the Lord. Just as God went after the Israelites in Egyptian bondage, He sought you and me out of the depths of sin, and we are, in turn, to pursue Him. God wants us to know Him intimately through spending time with Him, talking with Him, learning His ways and His character, and feasting on His Word. Are you truly seeking to know God?

The words from God to Hosea are true today: *"My people are destroyed for lack of knowledge"* (Hosea 4:6). High suicide and divorce rates among Christians, broken homes, fractured churches, wayward children…the list goes on. Too often professed Christians live defeated lives because they haven't breathed the air of eternal truth that comes from drawing near and understanding God's ways. We may feel conviction in our spirits, and so we run to do a good deed to relieve the stress on our hearts. But God, first and foremost, desires we sit down and get to know Him. God has said, *"For I desire mercy and not sacrifice, and the knowledge of God more than burnt offerings"* (Hosea 6:6 NKJV).

Just as I thought I knew Tricia before actually spending time with her, we can fool ourselves into thinking we have enough knowledge of God to say we truly know Him. God sees through our half-hearted attempts and superficial knowledge. The Scripture said of the Hebrew children's self-deception, *"Israel will cry to Me, 'My God, we know You!'"* (Hosea 8:2 NKJV). Just as He knew the Israelites' lips did not voice the truth in their hearts, He is keenly aware of our actual level of intimacy with Him.

Love-Letter Bouquet

Like Gomer and many of God's people in the Old Testament, we often struggle with consistency in our faithfulness. Read Hosea 6:4. Write a prayer for God's mercy and help for days when you find your faithfulness fading away like the early morning dew:

HELPING OTHERS KNOW HIM

Jesus performed His first miracle at a marriage celebration in Cana of Galilee (John 2:1). After the host (the groom's father) ran out of wine, Jesus transformed several containers of water into wine. The master of ceremonies complimented the groom's father on the "choice" wine that replaced the cheaper wine (John 2:10). Verse 11 tells the effect the miracle had on the disciples: *"He thus revealed his glory, and his disciples put their faith in him."* Suddenly these disciples, who'd known Jesus a short time, saw who He really was. Their shallow steps of faith grew into intimate knowledge.

The Lord's creation does not naturally know Him. John's Gospel records: *"He was in the world, and the world was made through Him, and the world did not know Him"* (1:10 NKJV). The word used here in the Greek, *ginosko*, has to do with knowing in a deeper sense, fully understanding through progressive studying. It's the same word used to convey the idea of a husband "knowing" his wife in a personal and intimate way. God's desire is for you and me to know Him very personally. *"Come now, you and I, Let us know, let us pursue the knowledge of the Lord"* (Hosea 6:3 NKJV).

Love-Letter Bouquet

Read John 1:35–51. What was the disciples' reaction when Jesus asked them to follow Him? Have you already made that commitment?

How can you step out in deeper faith to follow Him this week?

One tragedy of ungodly families in David's day was *"their maidens had no wedding songs"* (Psalm 78:63; see surrounding verses as well). How can you help others have faith in Christ so they can be invited to the wedding feast of the Lamb in heaven?

Reflections

How can you encourage your sisters in Christ in their pursuit of the knowledge of God?

ENJOYING THE ETERNAL WEDDING FEAST

John wrote his account of the wedding feast, or the marriage supper, of the Lamb: Jesus, the Bridegroom, sits on a throne, His bride beside Him. When you and I join Him in heaven, we'll be worthy to participate in the marriage supper without restraint. No earthly deadlines, difficult people, sinful behavior, or messy irritations will interfere with our joy; we'll join other Christians in eternal celebration! Jesus will *"wipe every tear from their eyes. There will be no more death or mourning or crying or pain"* (Revelation 21:4).

Love-Letter Bouquet

Read John's account of the wedding feast of the Lamb in Revelation 22:17. Who is the bride?

God says, *"The Spirit and the bride say, 'Come!' And let him who hears say, 'come!'"* (Revelation 22:17). As Jesus's bride, will *you* give the invitation to the celebration? How?

Read Revelation 22:17b. Who is the thirsty person in this verse? If you're spiritually thirsty, what should you do? According to this verse, what should you *wish*, or *will*, to do?

Compare this verse to Revelation 3:20. What happens after you open the door?

Reflections

As your contemplate your Bridegroom's love letters in Scripture, prayerfully write your final thoughts and allow Him to whisper personal words of encouragement in your ear.

As we've seen from Scriptures in earlier chapters of this book, God explains His extended metaphor from Genesis through Revelation: that Jesus Christ is the Bridegroom and we, the church of Christ, join Him as His bride as He calls us to enter a celebration of our union at the marriage feast in heaven. John describes *"A great multitude...shouting: 'Hallelujah! For our Lord God Almighty reigns. Let us rejoice and be glad and give him glory! For the wedding of the Lamb has come, and his bride has made herself ready'"* (Revelation 19:6–7).

PRAYER

Thank You, Lord, for bringing us into relationship with You. Thank you for the future marriage feast of the Lamb. Forgive us when we flippantly say we know You; we can never know you enough! Help us grow deeper in our understanding of Your mind and heart—as we seek intimacy with You daily.

INSIGHTS

HINTS OF THE FEAST TO COME

One starry night in Alabama, my church's witnessing teams tried a new adventure: going door-to-door. In one apartment building we presented the gospel to a shy Buddhist, a busy Methodist mother, and a friendly Mexican couple. Finally an older couple, the Jacksons, invited us in. There was no mistaking their Christianity! They immediately told us of their personal conversions and how they depended on Jesus to provide comfort and faith every day. They overflowed with the Holy Spirit!

"How long do you think we've been married?" they asked. We guessed 50 years.

"Nope! Two weeks!" This Christian widow and widower had just returned from their honeymoon! When they asked us about home states, I mentioned South Carolina.

"Used to know a guy from there," Mr. Jackson said. "Drove my old bus...dropped him off for weekends at his house before I went on home to Virginia." He smiled. "I heard he died years ago. Uh...Martin."

"I was a Martin before I married," I said.

"This Martin was in the navy with me."

"My father was in the navy."

"Oh, yeah? I was in the motor pool. Worked on jeeps."

"My father was in a motor pool!"

Mr. Jackson ran out of the room. In a few moments he returned, pulling a photo out of a cigar box. There they were: he and my father in their younger days with navy-blue bell bottoms and white naval hats tilted at a saucy angle.

"I have a photo at my house exactly like that," I said. "This man on the right is my father!"

"You're Martin's daughter?"

"Yes, and Daddy's still alive!"

We laughed; we hugged; we cried together.

In a few weeks, my father and mother reunited with his Christian buddy and met his new wife. The Martins and Jacksons reminisced about their years of experience as Christians who really *knew* the Lord, and celebrated friendships that would last through eternity. Surely the marriage feast in heaven will be something like that night of celebration—only greater! We will rejoice together in the Lord—laughing, dancing, and praising God with one another!

—Edna Ellison

PRAYER & PRAISE JOURNAL

A WEDDING INVITATION

From the first page of this book as you read about the choosing of the bride to the last chapter concluding in heaven with the celebration of the marriage supper, our focus has been on Christ, our Bridegroom. We hope you have learned several new facts and experienced more intimacy with your Savior. If you're not sure you know—or are known by—the Savior and therefore question whether you will be among the bride of Christ, you can *be sure* today by putting your life in His hands.

GOD'S FREE GIFT

How do we accept Christ's salvation? We do not earn it through good deeds or any other actions. Ephesians 2:8–9 says, *"For it is by grace you have been saved, through faith—and this is not from yourselves, it is the **gift** of God—not by works so that no one can boast"* [author's emphasis]. God provides our way to heaven as a free gift of His grace, through our faith, or trust, in Jesus as the risen, all-powerful Savior. Thank God for His free gift.

- Pray to God, admitting you are a sinner. Romans 3:23 says, *"All have sinned and fall short of the glory of God."* You're not alone. Every human being has sinned and is by nature a rebel against God. Confess your sins and ask God to forgive you.
- Acknowledge that Almighty God is holy, just, and must punish sin. No one would want to live in a world of anarchy, with right deeds unrewarded and wrong ones unpunished. Surely all people want a God of

justice to rule. Romans 6:23a says, *"For the wages of sin is death."* Thank God for being a just God as He judges the world.

💜 Thank God for sending His only Son, Jesus, to die in our place. Thank God for loving us enough to allow His Son to take the penalty of our sins, removing the barrier that separates us from Him.

💜 Accept the forgiveness He offers as you thank Him for saving us from death and eternal damnation. Romans 5:8 says, *"But God demonstrates his own love for us in this: While we were still sinners, Christ died for us."* Christ is now risen from the dead, alive today and seated at the right hand of the Father. He is mighty to save anyone who calls on Him.

💜 Go back and read the second half of Romans 3:23, *"but the gift of God is eternal life in Christ Jesus our Lord."* His gift is eternal life in Christ, the opposite of hell, sin, death, and eternal darkness without God. Close your prayer by telling God you *personally* accept His gift of eternal life! Ask Him to begin a deep personal relationship with you through His Spirit and rejoice in your salvation.

(For more on salvation, read John 3:1–21; Romans 10:9–13; and 1 John 5:11–15)

Satan may tempt you to doubt your salvation. Call on the Holy Spirit to sustain you during times of trouble and doubt. As the bride of Christ, depend on Him daily. Take assurance in 1 John 1:9, *"If we confess our sins, he is faithful and just and will forgive us our sins and purify us from all unrighteousness."*

Make sure you contact a local Christian pastor or Christian friend and join a local fellowship of believers near you. They will show you how to follow through on your commitment to Him with baptism and church membership.

Chosen and Cherished

Whether you are a vibrant, active Christian—rejoicing that you are the bride of Christ, anticipating heaven; or a long-time Christian who has wandered and now finds strength in your assurance of personal salvation and wants to grow in your intimacy with the Bridegroom; or a brand-new Christian who just accepted Jesus as your personal Savior a moment ago, our prayer is that this book has blessed you. May you accept your role in the church as the bride of Christ, growing ever closer to your Bridegroom, finding strength to face tomorrow!

If you'd like to let the authors know you have made a commitment to God through this Bible study, please contact us at http://www.wordsofjoy.org, www.ednaellison.com, or ksowell@comporium.net.

We, the authors, would like to celebrate with you as you finish the last page of this book by praising God and singing the words of an angel: *"'Come, gather together for the great supper of God'"* (Revelation 19:17). *"'Blessed are those who are invited to the wedding supper of the Lamb'"* (Revelation 19:9)! Anticipate the joy to come!

BASICS OF SALVATION

- 💜 We are all sinners.
- 💜 Our sin separates us from Holy God.
- 💜 We deserve punishment.
- 💜 God is just; He must punish sin.
- 💜 God is love; He wants to save us.
- 💜 We can't save ourselves.
- 💜 God sent Jesus to die for us, to take our punishment.
- 💜 He lovingly gives salvation as a free gift, by grace through faith.
- 💜 If we believe in the risen Lord, confessing our sins, accepting Him as our personal Savior, and desiring to be with Him for eternity, we are saved.
- 💜 There is no doubt we will go to heaven.

Leader's Guide
for Group Study
Facilitators and Mentors

Chapter 1:
Preliminaries
- ❤ Consider sending mock wedding invitations to invite participants to the study.
- ❤ Introduce the group to the concept of being chosen by Christ and cherished by Him as His bride (Revelation 21:9). Read the introductory material in this study together as appropriate.

Getting to Know You Activities
- ❤ As an icebreaker, ask participants to tell one person a unique thing that happened at their weddings. Then ask them to compare contemporary wedding elements to the elements of ancient weddings.
- ❤ Discuss each step in the modern and traditional weddings. Then, using a flip chart or dry-erase board, ask small groups to make a timeline of the ancient wedding elements and then a timeline of weddings today. (For instance, how long did it take to find your wedding dress? How do wedding planners organize processions before a wedding today?)

Closing
- ❤ Summarize the main points of the chapter, ending with 2 Corinthians 1:20. Give them a taste of the chapters to come.
- ❤ Lead in prayer, thanking God for His overall plan for you, the Church, the bride of Christ, thanking Him for the beautiful wedding imagery in the Bible and your faithfulness as His bride.

- Close with these words: *"Let us rejoice and be glad and give him the glory!... Blessed are those who are invited to the wedding supper of the Lamb!"* (Revelation 19:7–9).
- In advance, assign participants to complete the Love-Letter Bouquet questions in chapter 2.

Follow-up
Invite other women you are acquainted with to the wedding supper of the Lamb, food for the spirit and soul, at next week's study.

CHAPTER 2:
Preliminaries
Start the study by asking participants which Love-Letter Bouquet was the most meaningful to them.

Getting to Know You Activities
- As an icebreaker, ask participants to tell another person about an experience involving love-note promises that proved false or flowers that faded too soon.
- Ask, "How do flowers symbolize earthly love?"
- Continue to discuss participants' answers to each Love-Letter Bouquet question.
- Ask someone to tell about a time in which she realized God took delight in her.

Closing
- Summarize the section on avoiding anxiety in life. Ask each participant to join you in a quiet time of closing. Ask each one to listen to God's whisper.
- Lead in prayer, using the model at the end of the study.
- Assign participants to read chapter 3, answering all the Love-Letter Bouquet questions.

Follow-up
Establish a daily quiet time with God. Share with others in the group how you do your quiet time. Ask for their experiences and creative ideas, as well as their challenges.

CHAPTER 3:
Preliminaries
Open with prayer, thanking God for the sacrifice He has made for each participant.

Getting to Know You Activities
- ❤ As an icebreaker, ask participants to explain to two people near them how they think the traditions of *dowry* and *dower* play out today.
- ❤ Discuss all the Love-Letter Bouquet questions, especially those that pertain to Hebrew words that might need explanations from the chapter.
- ❤ Divide into small groups. Following the outline of benefits in the section "Power in the Blood," ask participants to share their personal understanding and experience of the listed benefits of the blood sacrifice of the Incarnate Lord. Share some of these insights with the large group.
- ❤ Ask participants to share what they learned from "The Rest of the Story" segment.

Closing
- ❤ Summarize the main points of the chapter, including the sidebar.
- ❤ Lead in prayer, using the prayer provided.
- ❤ Assign participants to read chapter 4, answering all the Love-Letter Bouquet questions.

Follow-up
Make a personal call or write an email asking participants if they have any questions about the power in the blood of Christ or any other concept in the first three studies.

CHAPTER 4:
Preliminaries
Open with prayer, thanking God for the cup of acceptance He has offered each participant.

Getting to Know You Activities

❤ As an icebreaker, ask for married volunteers to tell how their husbands proposed. Compare those to the experience of Joy and Wayne. Discuss all the Love-Letter Bouquet questions and contemplate Christ's sacrifice for us.

❤ Using material in this chapter, ask small-group participants to divide a flip chart or dry-erase board: on one side list the characteristics of the cup of our Bridegroom. On the other side, list characteristics of the cup of the bride of Christ. Use personal illustrations as you discuss these.

❤ Discuss what it would take for participants to live their lives with more joy.

Closing

❤ Summarize the main points of the chapter, including the important decisions made by brides and grooms and spiritual decisions made by the Church, the bride of Christ.

❤ Read the ending poem in the sidebar and then lead in prayer, using the prayer provided.

❤ Assign participants to read chapter 5, answering all the Love-Letter Bouquet questions.

Follow-up

❤ Lead the group in Communion by candlelight. (If this could pose a problem in your setting, clear the plan with your pastor or church board).

❤ Alternative: Sit together as a group at the next Communion observed in your church.

CHAPTER 5:
Preliminaries

Open with prayer, thanking God for the gifts he has given each participant.

Getting to Know You Activities

- 💜 As an icebreaker, ask participants to explain to the person sitting on their right how they would feel if they were in Rebekah's situation (Genesis 24).
- 💜 Discuss all the Love-Letter Bouquet questions, especially those that pertain to spiritual gifts.
- 💜 Using material in this chapter, ask small group participants to list the spiritual gifts on a flip chart or a dry-erase board.
- 💜 If possible, preorder a spiritual gifts inventory, encourage participants to take it, and then share their findings with the group. Or simply discuss the gifts listed in the text and ask participants to tell gifts they see in others or help each person find one or more gifts she can see in herself.
- 💜 Ask group members to list how their gifts can be used for the common good of the church.
- 💜 Discuss the gifts other family members may have (especially husbands).

Closing

- 💜 Summarize the main points of the chapter, including the irrevocability of God's call and His gifts.
- 💜 Lead in prayer, using the prayer provided.
- 💜 Assign participants to read Chapter 6.

Follow-up

Find a way to use a spiritual gift you have discovered in yourself for the good of your church or community.

CHAPTER 6:
Preliminaries

Open with prayer, asking God to help all participants watch for Christ's coming and welcome Him into their lives.

Getting to Know You Activities

♥ As an icebreaker, ask each participant to choose a friend and identify today's idols, using the definition in the "Remaining Faithful" segment. List these idols and share with the group.

♥ Discuss all the Love-Letter Bouquet questions, especially those that pertain to faithfulness in today's Christian.

♥ Ask small-group participants to list contemporary ideas about who God is. What are the problems in these views?

♥ Discuss how we can "make ourselves ready" for Christ since we don't know when He will come.

Closing

♥ Summarize the main points of the chapter, including ways we can be found faithful while waiting.

♥ Ask a another person to lead in prayer, using the prayer provided. (Talk with them about this before the group begins.)

♥ Assign participants to read Chapter 7.

Follow-up

Draw names and ask each participant to write a short note to their chosen group member encouraging her to live expectantly, pondering the goodness of the Bridegroom each day and hour.

CHAPTER 7:
Preliminaries

♥ Ask participants to bring their wedding dresses or a wedding photo.

♥ Optional: If possible, ask someone from another area or culture to tell about her wedding dress (e.g., red or other colors).

♥ Begin the Bible study by reading Revelation 19:7–8 (in a Love-Letter Bouquet question).

Getting to Know You Activities
- 💜 As an icebreaker, ask participants to share, with someone next to them, one interesting thing regarding their wedding dress. Ask several volunteers to share these with the large group.
- 💜 Discuss the words in parentheses in Revelation 19:8. Describe the *"righteous acts of the saints"* in today's church. (Explain that "saints" are ordinary Christians.)
- 💜 Ask pre-assigned persons to tell how several of the Scriptures in the section entitled "Pure and Spotless" apply to today's women.
- 💜 Discuss other Love-Letter Bouquet questions, especially those that pertain to the symbolism of physical wedding garments as compared to spiritual garments we "wear" for our Groom.

Closing
- 💜 If possible, ask someone to sing "How Beautiful Is the Body of Christ" (by Twila Paris). Or play a recording of this song.
- 💜 Ask someone to close the discussion time with a challenge for every participant to seek and wear the clothing of righteousness.
- 💜 Ask participants to stand in a circle and read aloud the closing prayer at the end of this chapter.
- 💜 Assign participants to read Chapter 8 and answer all the Love-Letter Bouquet questions.

Follow-up
- 💜 Give each participant an index card and ask her to record examples of people wearing or not wearing their "spiritual clothes" of modesty, purity, and strength this week.
- 💜 Alternate: Go shopping together and look for items of modesty versus outrageous or immodest items. Determine what spiritual garments you're wearing each day and decide to choose only clothes of righteousness.

CHAPTER 8:

Preliminaries

- 💜 Open with prayer, asking God to help all participants focus on their Groom, Jesus Christ.
- 💜 Ask all participants from the last Bible study to share what they found and recorded on their index cards about dressing in righteousness.

Getting to Know You Activities

- 💜 As an icebreaker, ask participants to chose one other woman and compare their answers to the matching activity in the Love-Letter Bouquet on page 96. Ask them to write down any questions they have about the Scriptures in the matching activity.
- 💜 Discuss all the Love-Letter Bouquet questions with the group. Ask participants to share other points of interest in the chapter.
- 💜 Share ways to avoid being misdirected in our walk or distracted by appearances, customs, or other "things." Share ways to keep from losing our joy as overstressed brides often do.
- 💜 Ask each participant to brainstorm with a partner and compose together seven blessings for a Christian preparing to be the bride of Christ. Exchange the blessings with another duo.

Closing

- 💜 Ask each participant to join you in vows of renewal of your love for Christ.
- 💜 Close by praying for participants, using the prayer at the end of the chapter.
- 💜 Assign participants to read Chapter 9.

Follow-up

- 💜 Pray for a renewal in each heart and a personal relationship with Jesus.

CHAPTER 9:

Preliminaries

Open in prayer, praying especially for each participant to experience spiritual intimacy with Christ during this study.

Getting to Know You Activities

💜 As an icebreaker, ask pairs to role play introducing themselves to Jesus (per Love-Letter Bouquet activity on page 106). Ask volunteers to read their introduction of themselves to Jesus or perform their role playing before the large group.

💜 Discuss all the Love-Letter Bouquet questions and points of personal reflection in this chapter.

💜 Divide into small groups and ask each group to list (on a flip chart or dry-erase board) the stages of courtship in this chapter. Under each stage, list the main points or ideas that touched participants as they studied the chapter.

💜 Close the activity by reading Joy's words near the end of this chapter. "When I realized that nothing I ever could do would cause God to love me *any less or any more*, this recognition transformed my life, too." Encourage participants to share their personal stories of being transformed by Christ.

Closing

💜 If someone in the group has had an unexpected change in her spiritual life similar to Joy's story ending the chapter ("I know this story is true. I was the Sunday School teacher"), ask that person to share with the group.

💜 Enlarge and display the Vance Havner quote in the sidebar. Challenge participants to avoid being "subnormal."

💜 Close in prayer, using the prayer at the end of the chapter.

💜 Assign participants to read Chapter 10.

Follow-up
- Challenge participants to promise God they won't be "subnormal" this week.
- Alternate: Invite someone from outside your group to join you for the last study at the next meeting.

Chapter 10:

Preliminaries
- Ask everyone to name her favorite "closing" or "last" (last day on a hard job, last day of school, closing of a mortgage loan, and others).
- Lead in a celebratory prayer for completion of the Bible study. Thank God for His Presence.

Getting to Know You Activities
- As an icebreaker, ask each participant to share her "best party memory ever."
- On a flip chart or dry-erase board, list some family traditions (habits, stories, creating a family tree, and so on). Mention family understanding and intimacy. ("It's a family thing!") Suggest since they are all part of the family of God, they can become more intimate with Christ (and each other) as they celebrate the spiritual marriage feast with Him through Bible study, prayer, meditation, and church fellowship.
- Discuss Love-Letter Bouquet questions, especially those that compare the story of Gomer and Hosea to contemporary responses to Christ.
- Ask for other points or ideas of interest from any chapter that need reviewing.

Closing

- ♥ Ask participants to share their favorite part of the side-bar story. How does the celebration of the Martins and Jacksons compare to the celebration at the marriage feast in heaven?
- ♥ Join hands, and ask for short sentence prayers. Close with the prayer at the end of the chapter.

Follow-up

- ♥ Be sure everyone reads the conclusion and understands it. Tell participants you and/or other strong Christians will remain after the study to pray with anyone who does not already have an intimate relationship with her Bridegroom, Jesus Christ.
- ♥ Bring refreshments and have a simple marriage feast before or after this last Bible study.

Other
New Hope Bible Studies
for Women

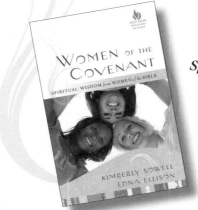

Women of the Covenant
Spiritual Wisdom from Women of the Bible
Kimberly Sowell and Edna Ellison
ISBN-10: 1-59669-270-7
ISBN-13: 978-1-59669-270-1

Face-to-Face with Naomi and Ruth
Together for the Journey
Janet Thompson
ISBN 10: 1-59669-253-7
ISBN 13: 978-1-59669-253-4

Face-to-Face with Mary and Martha
Sisters in Christ
Janet Thompson
ISBN 10: 1-59669-254-5
ISBN 13: 978-1-59669-254-1

Available in bookstores everywhere

For information about these books or any New Hope product,
visit www.newhopepublishers.com.